ROAD TRIP USA

Jamie Jensen

Contents

APPALACHIAN TRAIL

This driving route parallels the hiking trail, from the top of New England to the heart of Dixie, taking you through continuous natural beauty – without the sweat, bugs, or blisters.

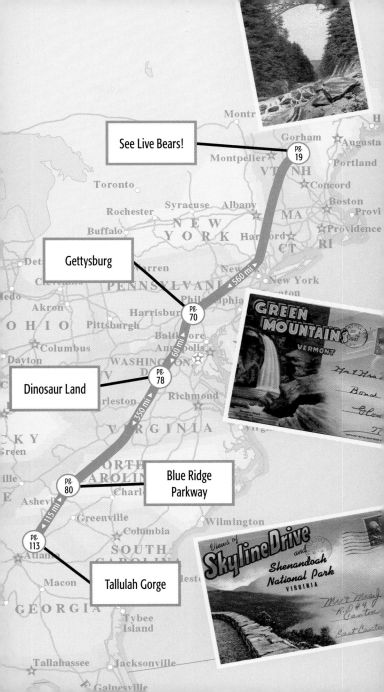

See Live Bears!
pg. 19

Gettysburg
pg. 70

Dinosaur Land
pg. 78

Blue Ridge Parkway
pg. 80

Tallulah Gorge
pg. 113

560 mi.

60 mi.

350 mi.

115 mi.

GREEN MOUNTAINS
VERMONT

Views of Skyline Drive and Shenandoah National Park
VIRGINIA

Between the North Woods of Maine and Atlanta, Georgia

The longest and best-known hiking trail in the country, the **Appalachian Trail** winds from the north woods of Maine all the way south to Georgia. While you won't earn the same kudos driving as you would by walking, the following scenic roads come very close to paralleling the pedestrian route, taking you through the almost continuous natural beauty without the sweat and blisters. Best of all, this driving route follows magnificently scenic two-lane roads all the way from the top of New England to the heart of Dixie, running past a wealth of fascinating towns and historic sites.

The Appalachian landscape holds some of the wealthiest, and some of the most needy, areas in the entire country. These contrasting worlds often sit within a few miles of one another: Every resort and retirement community seems to have its alter-ego as a former mill town, now as dependent upon tourism as they once were upon the land and its resources.

After an extended sojourn through the rugged and buggy wilds of northern **Maine,** where the hikers' route winds to the top of Mt. Katahdin, our Appalachian Trail driving tour reaches an early high point atop windswept Mt. Washington in the heart of **New Hampshire's Presidential Range.** From these 6,000-foot peaks, the tallest mountains in New England and some of the hardest and most durable rocks on earth, the route winds through **Vermont's Green Mountains,** taking in the idyllic charms of rural New England, with its summer homes and liberal-arts college communities. Beyond the **Berkshires,** the summer destination of the Boston and New York culture vultures and intelligentsia for most of two centuries, towns become even more prissy and pretty as we approach within commuting distance of New York City.

Skirting the Big Apple, our route ducks down through the **Delaware Water Gap** to enter the suddenly industrial Lehigh Valley, former land of coal and steel that's now struggling to find an economic replacement. South of here, we pass through the heart of the world-famous **Pennsylvania Dutch Country,** where the simple life is under the onslaught of package tourism.

South from Pennsylvania, nearly to the end of the route in **Georgia,** the Appalachian Trail runs through continuous nature, with barely a city to be seen. Starting with Virginia's **Shenandoah National Park,** then following the **Blue Ridge Parkway** across the breathtaking mountains of western **North Carolina,** it's All-American scenic highway all the way, with recommended detours east and west to visit such fascinating historic

Though the Appalachian Trail runs within **day-hiking** distance of over 50 million people, most of the route is intensely solitary—only some 200 people manage to hike the entire 2,144-mile trail each year.

sights as Thomas Jefferson's home, Monticello, outside Charlottesville, Virginia; the most opulent mansion in America, Asheville's Biltmore; the real-life town that inspired TV's *Mayberry RFD*—Mount Airy, North Carolina; or the white water featured in the film *Deliverance,* north Georgia's Chattooga River.

All in all, the Appalachian Trail is an amazing drive, whether or not you come for fall color.

NEW HAMPSHIRE

"Live Free or Die" is the feisty motto of tiny New Hampshire, the state that hits the national limelight every four years when its political primaries launch the horse race for the White House. During the presidential campaign's opening stretch, locals have to turn into hermits to avoid having their votes solicited by every candidate running and their opinions polled by every reporter. Some of New Hampshire's million residents take the state's motto to heart, however, and when you see the ruggedness of the landscape you'll appreciate how easy it is to find isolation from the madding crowd.

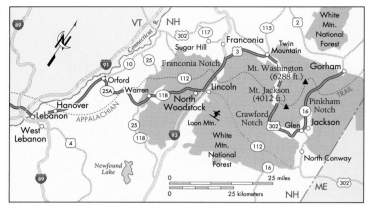

Despite its apparent brevity, the route across New Hampshire provides a hearty sampling of the topographic spectrum from its start at New England's highest peak, Mt. Washington, to neighboring Vermont amid the rolling farmland of the Connecticut River Valley.

Mt. Washington

The star attraction of the White Mountains' Presidential Range, 6,288-foot **Mt. Washington** stands head and shoulders above every other peak in New England. East of the Mississippi, only Mt. Mitchell in North Carolina's Blue Ridge and Clingman's Dome in Tennessee's Great Smokies are taller. Despite its natural defenses—such as notoriously fierce storms that arise without warning—Mt. Washington is accessible to an almost unfortunate degree. The **Mount Washington Auto Road** (May to mid-Oct. daily, weather permitting; $23 car and driver, $8 each additional adult; 603/466-3988) was first opened for carriages in 1861, earning it the nickname "America's Oldest Man-Made Tourist Attraction." It still switchbacks up the eastern side, climbing some 4,700 feet in barely eight miles. A marvel of engineering, construction, and maintenance, the Mount Washington Auto Road offers a great variety of impressions of the mountain and wonderful views from almost every turn.

Although clear-day views from the summit of Mt. Washington are amazing, 9 days out of 10 the summit is socked in and cold, and snow can fall any month of the year.

If the weather's clear, you can see the Atlantic Ocean from the top of the mountain; in summer, mornings tend to be clearer, and

Severe Weather on Mt. Washington

A mountain barely over 6,000 feet hardly deserves the same respect as Mount Everest (29,029 feet), or even Mount McKinley (20,320 feet), yet people die from exposure on the slopes of New Hampshire's Mt. Washington all the same. Easy access invites complacency and a tendency to ignore trailside warnings advising retreat if you're unprepared for bad weather. But do respect the facts of nature: Simply put, the Presidential Range of the White Mountains experiences some of the worst weather in the world, rivaling both Antarctica and the Alaska-Yukon ranges for consistently raw and bone-numbing combinations of gale-force winds, freezing temperatures, and precipitation. Lashings by 100-mph winds occur year-round on Mt. Washington, whose summit holds the title for highest sustained wind speed on the face of the planet (231 mph in April 1934). Cloudy days outnumber clear ones on the peak, where snowstorms can strike any month of the year, and even in the balmiest summer months the average high temperature at the summit hovers around 50°F. Compounding the weather's potential severity is its total unpredictability: A day hike begun with sunblock and short sleeves can end up in driving rain and temperatures just 10 degrees above freezing—or worse, in a total whiteout above tree line—even as a group of hikers a couple miles away on a neighboring peak enjoys lunch under blue skies and warm breezes.

The bottom line is, listen to what your mother always told you: Be careful, and don't take chances. Learn to recognize and prevent hypothermia. Figure out how to read your trail maps and use your compass *before* you get caught in pelting sleet above tree line. Better to feel foolish packing potentially unnecessary wool sweaters and rain gear for a hike in July than to have your name added to the body count.

The first automobile ascent of Mt. Washington was made in 1899 by none other than **F. O. Stanley**, piloting one of his namesake **Stanley Steamers.**

historic Tip Top House at the summit of Mt. Washington

sunny afternoons turn cloudy and stormy on the summit, complete with lightning and thunder. At the top, be prepared for winter weather any time of year (it can and does snow here every month of the year), and be sure to have a look inside the Summit House, which has displays on the historic hotels and taverns that have graced the top over the years. Visited by hundreds of people every day throughout the summer, since the 1850s the summit of Mt. Washington has sprouted a series of restaurants and hotels—even a daily newspaper. The most evocative remnant of these is the tiny **Tip Top House,** "the oldest mountaintop hostelry in the world," still open for tours, if not food and drink (which is available in the Summit House cafeteria).

In New England, locals call their highways **"routes,"** and we've followed suit, using Route as a generic term (Route 100 for example, rather than Hwy-100). The Interstates (I-93) and federal highways (US-3) are abbreviated as usual.

Cyclists and runners regularly race each other up the road to the summit, but there is another easy ride to the top: the **Mount Washington Cog Railway,** which climbs slowly but surely on its steam-powered, coal-fired way, straight up and down the mountain's western slope from Bretton Woods.

Pinkham Notch

South from the foot of the Mount Washington Auto Road, Route 16 passes through Pinkham Notch, a mostly undeveloped stretch of the White Mountains lined by forests and a few ski areas. About four miles south of the Auto Road is the area's outdoorsy Grand Central Station: the **Pinkham Notch Camp.** Operated by the venerable Appalachian Mountain Club (AMC), the year-round trailhead facility offers topographical maps, guidebooks, weather updates, and precautionary advice, as well as limited gear. The camp also offers snacks, a cafeteria, a 24-hour hikers' pack room with bathrooms and showers, scheduled shuttle van service, and the **Joe Dodge Lodge** (about $65/person bed and board; 603/466-2727), a modern hostel with shared bunk rooms, a few private doubles, and great views from the library.

North to Mt. Katahdin

North and east of Mt. Washington, the Appalachian Trail runs through one of its toughest sections, rambling through Mahoosuc Notch into Maine, then passing through Grafton Notch State Park. There are no real roads anywhere near here, so drivers wanting a quick taste of this impenetrable country will have to join US-2 for the drive through Gorham and Bethel, then wind along the Bear River on scenic Route 26. Beyond Grafton Notch, the hikers' Appalachian Trail passes through ever more extensive wilderness, with fewer services (and many more mosquitoes and black flies!) the closer you get to the trail's northern finish, atop **Mt. Katahdin.**

Though the hiking trail and the nearest roads are like strands of a double helix, both routes take you through some memorable country, especially around Rangeley Lakes and Moosehead Lake, in the deep Maine woods.

Mt. Washington Valley: Jackson

Dropping sharply away to the south of Pinkham Notch is the

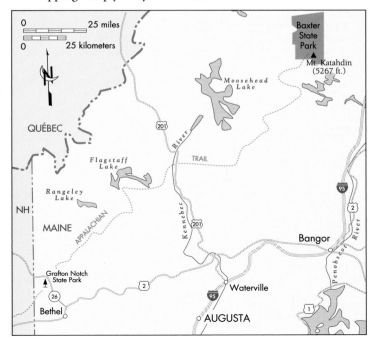

To park a car at any trailhead in the White Mountains National Forest, you'll need to buy a **pass** from one of the information centers; these passes cost about $5 and are good for seven days.

Ellis River, along whose banks sits the northern gateway to the Mt. Washington valley, resort-dominated **Jackson** (pop. 678). Given the number of lodgings among the attractive century-old clapboard homes, it seems the principal village occupation is innkeeper. The quantity of porches, gables, and chimneys hint at standard country B&B charms: lazy breakfasts in summer, nooks and crannies brimming with roses, and crackling fires in your room at night. A covered bridge beside Route 16, taverns filled with antiques, and winter sleigh rides complete Jackson's postcard image of Merry Olde New England.

The Jackson area is not only pretty but also has a couple of northern New Hampshire's best places to eat, drink, and sleep. At the junction of Route 16 and Route 16B, the **Shannon Door Pub** (603/383-4211) is usually just the right side of crowded—full of skiers, hikers, and other hungry folks enjoying hearty food, good beers, and frequent live folksy, Celtic-tinged music in a jovial setting. In business for nearly 60 years, the pub was a main character in John Sayles' first film, *The Return of the Secaucus Seven.* The grand hotel in Jackson is the stately **Wentworth** (603/383-9700) at the heart of the village, welcoming travelers since it was established back in 1880.

Glen

A half mile south of Jackson along Route 16 or Route 16A you pass the picturesque Jackson Covered Bridge, where the two alternates rejoin at the north edge of tiny **Glen.** In the short stretch between the bridge and the junction with US-302, Glen has one of the more concentrated barrages of roadside clutter in the White Mountains. Glen is best known not for hiking or sightseeing but as home to the children's theme park **Story Land** (daily in summer only; $24, under 4 free; 603/383-4186), where among its many playfully designed and carefully coifed acres, the highlights include a

boat ride, a raft ride, and a fake fiberglass cow that gives fake milk when you squeeze its fake udders.

A half mile south of Storyland, Route 16 links up with US-302 at a cluster of shops where the **Red Parka Pub** (603/383-4344), a jolly, moderate-to-inexpensive place to eat and drink, has live music most weekend nights.

North Conway

If you're overdue for a little retail therapy you might consider continuing south on Route 16 from the US-302 junction toward **North Conway** (pop. 2,069), one of the cornerstones of New England's factory-outlet circuit. City dwellers be warned: Horrible flashbacks to your commute may result if you venture into the shopping mall zone, where half-hour (or longer) crawls along a five-mile stretch of highway are not unheard-of on holidays, weekends, and afternoons, or during summers, springs, and autumns.

Besides factory-outlet stores, North Conway is also home to New Hampshire's most popular scenic railroad, running steam engines throughout summer and during the fall color season. Based out of Conway's downtown depot, the **Conway Scenic Railroad** ($15 and up depending on trip; 603/356-5251) runs historic trains south to Conway, through Bartlett, and all the way to Crawford Notch via the historic Frankenstein Trestle, with special excursions available in addition to these frequent trips.

Although all the tourists may well drive you away from North Conway, there are some good places to eat along Route 16, like **Elvio's Pizza,** 2888 White Mountain Highway (603/356-3208), where you can get slices or full pies, submarine sandwiches, and big salads, plus wine and beer. During the day, the place to eat home-style breakfasts or great burgers is family-friendly **Peaches,** 2506 White Mountain Highway (603/356-5860).

There are lots of accommodations on and off Route 16, from old cabin courts to anodyne motels, but the most interesting place has to be the **Cranmore Inn** ($85 and up; 603/356-5502),

If you can turn a blind eye to all the retail frenzy, North Conway's central park offers one of the **best views of Mt. Washington,** and the **baseball diamond** here hosts some pretty intense games.

Just over the Maine border, about 10 miles east of North Conway via US-302, the town of **Fryeburg** hosts a weeklong **agricultural fair** during the first week in October that's one of the most popular in New England—packed with tractor pulls, horse racing, lots of music, even a pig scramble (a contest, not an egg dish).

a quick walk east of Route 16 at 80 Kearsarge Street, which has been welcoming travelers since 1863.

Conway

Conway, five miles down Route 16 from North Conway at the south end of the scenic railroad line, is a nicer, littler town, with a couple of restaurants, a post office, and the very clean and very friendly **HI-White Mountains Hostel** ($25 per person, $60 private rooms; 603/447-1001), in the heart of town at 36 Washington Street. If you have your doubts about hostelling, this place is sure to dispel them; run as a sustainable living center, it's as clean as it is serene, and besides saving money staying here, you're apt to meet like-minded fellow travelers over breakfast or relaxing in the game room.

Up in the hills above Conway, off Route 16 one mile south of the Kancamagus Highway at the edge of the White Mountains National Forest, the **Darby Field Inn** ($125 and up; 603/447-2181) is a B&B open year-round for skiing, hiking, and great après-outdoors meals.

Kancamagus Highway

Running east–west from Conway over the mountains to Lincoln, the 34-mile **Kancamagus Highway** (Route 112) is one of the most incredible drives in the White Mountains. Much shorter and a lot less traveled than the prime tourist route along US-302 and US-3 through Crawford and Franconia Notches, the Kanc, as it's often called, takes you up and over the crest of the peaks, giving grand vistas over an almost completely undeveloped landscape—great for fall-color leaf-peeping. Fall is definitely prime time for the drive, but any time of year (except maybe winter, when it can be a bit hairy) it's a lovely trip, lined by lupines in early summer and raging waterfalls in the spring.

Near the midpoint of the Kanc, the

Fall foliage is at its best when warm clear days are followed by cold nights that stop the essential pigment-producing sugars from circulating out of the leaves. Sugar production is low on cloudy days, when warm nights allow the sugars to disperse before the brightest colors are produced. For **New Hampshire Fall Foliage Reports** (Sept. and Oct. only), call 800/258-3608.

Russell Colbath Historic House dates from the early 1800s and now houses a small museum (daily 9 AM–4 PM; free) with exhibits describing the lives of the White Mountains' early settlers. From the house, a short loop trail explores the effects loggers had on this region in the 1890s, when everything you see along the Kanc (and most everywhere else) was devastated by clear-cuts.

The name Kancamagus honors the local Indian chief who controlled the area when the first European settlers began arriving at the White Mountains in the 1680s. The roadway was not paved until 1964 and was declared a National Scenic Byway in 1989.

Three miles farther west, just east of the crest and an easy half-mile walk from the well-signed parking area, **Sabbaday Falls** is a lovely little waterfall roaring through a narrow gorge. In a series of noisy, splashing cascades, the river drops down through a polished pink granite gorge, barely 10 feet wide but surrounded by dense forest. It's an ideal picnic spot, and only 10–15 minutes from the road.

Crawford Notch

US-302 between Glen and Twin Mountain winds west around the southern flank of the Presidential Range, then heads north through **Crawford Notch,** another of the White Mountains' high passes and centerpiece of the **Crawford Notch State Park.** The road closely follows the Saco River through new-growth forest; the oaks and white pine of the lower valley give way to more birch and spruce as you gain elevation.

Crawford Notch offers good **day hikes** to various waterfalls and vantage points such as **Frankenstein Cliff,** named for an artist whose work helped popularize the White Mountains, and 200-foot **Arethusa Falls,** the state's highest waterfall.

The first known ascent of Mt. Washington was made in 1642 by **Darby Field** of Durham, New Hampshire, who historians believe followed a route near that of today's Crawford Path.

For ambitious and well-prepared hikers, the north end of Crawford Notch is the start of the oldest and perhaps grandest walking trail in the country, the eight-mile **Crawford Path** up towering Mt. Washington. A strenuous, demanding, and potentially dangerous route, the Crawford Path is also breathtakingly beautiful, and a walk along it gives an almost complete picture of the White

Parking along New Hampshire highways is **illegal,** so don't be tempted to leave your car beside the road while you take a hike up that nearby hill—you may return to find it's been towed to some town 20 miles away.

Mountains—sparkling brooks, fields of wildflowers, and glorious mountaintop panoramas.

Mount Washington Hotel and Cog Railway

North of Crawford Notch, the highway joins the Ammonoosuc River headwaters as they flow toward the Connecticut River, passing **Bretton Woods** and the access road for the Mount Washington Cog Railway. The giant **Mount Washington Hotel** ($195 and up; 800/258-0330) dominates the surrounding plain, its Victorian luxury no longer standing in such grand isolation below the peaks of the Presidentials now that a ski resort sits across the highway, and motels and condos squat around its skirts. Built at the turn of the 20th century by Pennsylvania Railroad tycoon Joseph Stickney, the Mount Washington Hotel received its most lasting recognition as host of the 1944 United Nations International Monetary Conference, the historic meeting of financiers from 44 nations that established the World Bank and chose the dollar as the global standard for international trade.

Climbing the mountains behind the hotel, the **Mount

Washington Cog Railway** was built in 1869 and has a maximum grade of 37.5 percent, surpassed by only one other non-funicular railway in the world, high up in the Swiss Alps. One cinder-spewing engine runs on coal, but others have been adapted to run on eco-friendly biodiesel. This historic "Railway to the Moon" takes over an hour to ratchet up the three-mile track to the often windy, cold summit. Trips ($60; 603/278-5404) run year-round; you can ride up and hike (or ski) back down.

Much more active and exciting than the slow chug up the cog railway is the **Bretton Woods Canopy Tour** ($15 and up) which takes you on a tour up into the top of the trees by way of cables, bridges, and ziplines.

Cannon Mountain, home slope of World Cup ski champion **Bode Miller,** was the location of the first aerial tram for skiers in the United States. One of the original aerial tram cars has been preserved among the many attractions at Clark's Trading Post, near Lincoln at the south end of Franconia Notch.

Franconia and Sugar Hill

Between Twin Mountain (at the junction of US-302 and US-3) and where US-3 merges with I-93, you'll find the aging face of the area's long association with tourism: a variety of motel courts and "housekeeping cottages" at least as old as you are. Despite their outward dowdiness, several make a virtue of the rustic, but given their prime location most are hardly the bargains you might hope for. More interesting and historic lodging may be had on a 200-acre working farm in **Franconia** (pop. 811), where, since 1899, the friendly Sherburn family's **Pinestead Farm Lodge,** on Route 116 south of town, has offered simple rooms and warm hospitality at reasonable rates ($50 and up with shared bath and kitchen; 603/823-8121).

Just west of Franconia on Route 117 in **Sugar Hill.** The township is aptly named: The sugarbush (a grove of sugar maples) on Hildex Maple Sugar Farm contributes its unforgettable essence to breakfasts at the very popular **Polly's Pancake Parlor.** Polly's is located in the farm's thrice-expanded 1830 carriage shed (daily 7 AM–2 PM; closed in winter; 603/823-5575). Warning: After trying real maple syrup, you may never be able to go back to Mrs. Butterworth's again.

The most famous farm in the vicinity is certainly the **Frost Place** ($5; 603/823-5510) on Route 116 south of the Franconia village intersection. Besides the 1.5-mile Poetry Trail and the displays of Robert Frost memorabilia from his 11-year residency here, there's a regular program of readings by the current poet-in-residence.

Franconia Notch

Franconia Notch is probably the most popular spot in the White Mountains, and, despite the numbers of visitors, it's a fantastic place to spend some time. I-93, the country's only two-lane Interstate, offers easy access; a host of attractions—an aerial tram, the state's own "little Grand Canyon," covered bridges, a powerful waterfall called the Flume, even a trading post with trained bears—make it a great place to linger. If you give yourself the time to hike around or just sit still by a mountain stream, you could easily spend a week or more enjoying it all.

The main draw in Franconia Notch used

The hikers' Appalachian Trail crosses the Franconia Notch Parkway and Pemi Trail at Whitehouse Bridge, in between the Basin and the Flume.

to be one of the most famous landmarks in New England: the **Old Man of the Mountain,** a series of five granite ledges 1,200 feet above the valley, which, when viewed from certain angles, seemed to resemble an old man's profile. After years of reconstructive surgery, being held together by epoxies and steel reinforcement, the Old Man came tumbling down on May 3, 2003.

Fortunately, the other well-known feature of Franconia Notch is still there: **The Flume** is a granite gorge, 15 feet wide and nearly 100 feet high, carved by roaring waters at the south end of the notch. To get there, head to the large **visitors center** (603/745-8391), pay the admission fee ($15), and take a short bus ride to near the start of the wooden boardwalk, which runs the length of the 800-foot-long gorge and ends up at the ear-pounding rumble of Avalanche Falls.

Though less famous than the Old Man and the Flume, in between the two sits another favorite Franconia Notch stop: **the Basin,** where a lovely waterfall in the thundering Pemigewassett River has polished a 25-foot-round pothole. Thoreau visited in the 1820s and thought it was remarkable; it's still a peaceful place to sit and picnic and be soothed by the natural white noise.

Take those **moose-crossing** signs seriously. Dozens of collisions occur annually, and you can bet your car won't fare too well if it hits an animal that weighs well over a half ton.

Clark's Trading Post

Just south of Franconia Notch along US-3, a barrage of deliciously tacky tourist attractions and old-fashioned roadside Americana awaits you. Well-maintained 1930s motor courts line the highway, setting the stage for one of New England's greatest Roadside Attractions: **Clark's Trading Post** (daily in summer; $18; 603/745-8913), where you can enjoy a slice of good ol' cornpone kitsch. At Clark's, you can ride on a genuine old wood-burning railroad over an authentic 1904 covered bridge (and be chased all the way by a hairy, hilarious Wolfman); admire an immaculate 1931 LaSalle in a vintage gas station; or tour a haunted mansion.

For the past 50 or so years, the main draw at Clark's has been the chance, according to the sign, to **See Live Bears!** House-trained black bears perform a series of entertaining tricks—rolling barrels, shooting basketballs through hoops, and riding scooters—and they clearly seem to enjoy their work (not to mention the ice cream cones they're rewarded with). The trainers and caretakers crack jokes and make wry comments about "bear facts" and how the animals are "bearly" able to behave themselves, but they smile and beam every time the bears do what they're supposed to, giving the performances a feel more akin to a school play than to a professional circus. Many of the bears are born and reared here at Clark's, and although they're captive, they have a much longer life expectancy than wild bears. Across from the enclosure where they perform you can pay respects to the graves of favorite bears who've performed here over the years. Spend any time at Clark's and you'll begin to realize that the bears are regarded as family members (albeit seven-foot-tall, 500-pound family members).

Clark's has been in business since 1928, when it was known as Ed Clark's Eskimo Dog Ranch, and everything about it is very much a family affair. More than a dozen Clarks and close relatives work here throughout the summer, doing everything from training and caring for the bears to making milk shakes. The bear shows at Clark's Trading Post start every two hours or so (roughly at noon, 2, and 4 PM), and you could happily spend most of a day here, making it well worth the price of admission. If you're just racing through, be sure to at least visit the gift shop, which is stocked with all the wonderfully tacky stuff (wind-up toys, funky postcards, snow domes, and the like) retro-minded road-trippers drive miles to find.

Lincoln and North Woodstock

Three miles south of Franconia Notch, tiny **North Woodstock** (pop. 700) is a good example of what White Mountains towns used to look like before vacation condos popped up like prairie dog colonies; neighboring **Lincoln** (pop. 1,229) is the portrait of "after." North Woodstock is a handful of mostly unpretentious businesses at the junction of US-3 and Route 112, while Lincoln seems to be nothing but a strip of ski-clothing stores, malls, and motels east of I-93 at

Lincoln sits at the west end of Route 112, the amazing Kancamagus Highway.

In case you're wondering what North Woodstock is north of, there is a much smaller hamlet called **Woodstock,** little more than a collection of cabins, about three miles south of North Woodstock along US-3.

the base of the Loon Mountain ski resort. When Loon's condo-covered foothills fill to capacity during fall and winter holidays, the weekend population can mushroom more than 20-fold to more than 30,000.

Diner fans will want to check out the **Sunny Day Diner** (closed Tues.; 603/745-4833), a stainless-steel 1950s icon at the north edge of North Woodstock on US-3. A classic breakfast and lunch place, the Sunny Day makes some fine French toast (including a deeply flavored banana variation that goes great with local maple syrup). The Sunny Day is just south of Clark's Trading Post.

Lost River Gorge

With five main roads and countless minor ones connecting the Franconia Notch area with the Connecticut River Valley, there are nearly endless ways to get between these two places while staying more or less on the path of the hikers' Appalachian Trail, which disappears into the woods for most of the way. All of the roads are partly pretty and partly yucky in about equal degrees, but one of the easiest to follow is Route 112, which runs west from North Woodstock along the Lost River, hopping over the crest and dropping down along the Wild Ammonusuc. The main stop along this route is the privately owned gorge known as the **Lost River** (daily mid-May–Oct.; $15; 603/745-8031), where you can explore the jumble of glaciated granite boulders that seem to swallow up the river, giving it its name. Many of the big, moss-covered boulders have been given names (Guillotine Rock and Lemon Squeezer, to name two), and you can see these (and smell the fragrant pine trees) from the comfort of a wooden boardwalk or go wild and explore some of the many caves formed by the huge piles of rocks.

Continuing west from Lost River Gorge, which sits at the top of Route 112's spectacular run through wild Kinsman Notch, the highway drops down into the Connecticut River watershed toward the Vermont town of Wells River, which happens to be home to the best truck stop in all New

You Can't Get There from Here

One of the first things first-time visitors to New England notice is its compact size: A crow flying 100 miles from almost any treetop outside of Maine will end up in the next state, if not Canada. But map distances bear absolutely no relation to travel time, thanks to the mountain ranges pitched up across northern New England. So if you're sitting in your motel room in New Hampshire or Vermont wondering how far to drive for dinner, look to towns north or south. As a rule these will share the same valley since the rivers and mountains are generally aligned north-to-south, like compass needles. In contrast, that next town to the east or west may as well be on the opposite side of the state so far as convenience is concerned: Whether winding along erratic streambeds or stitching their ways up the sides of passes between high peaks, east–west roads tend to be a slow grind in even the best weather, truly as tortuous as the wiggling lines on the map suggest. Heavy vehicles, cautious drivers, and foul weather make the going doubly difficult. Keep this in mind as you consider outings and side trips or you, too, will learn to say, "You can't get there from here."

England: the **P&H Truck Stop Cafe** (802/429-2141) at I-91 exit 17, where you can enjoy fine chowder, charbroiled cheeseburgers, and great pies—24 hours a day. After eating here, backtrack four miles to the river and follow scenic Route 10 along its east bank, winding south toward Hanover. A parallel route along the Vermont side of the river, along old US-5 through the town of Fairlee (which has a nice diner and a unique drive-in movie theater/motel), is another nice alternative to the I-91 freeway.

Route 10: North Haverhill and Lyme

While hikers along the Appalachian Trail have to struggle up and over several mountaintops, we drivers get to amble along a few miles to the west, following scenic Route 10 along the east banks of the lazy Connecticut River. Winding past pastures and cornfields, Route 10 is a nonstop pleasure to drive (or cycle); uneventful, perhaps, but giving seemingly endless pastoral views framed by white rail fences, occasional farmhouses, and the voluptuous

In case you're worried, Lyme, New Hampshire, is not the place the tick-borne disease was named for; that Lyme is in Connecticut. That said, you still need to be on the lookout for these devilish little creatures.

peaks that rise to the east and west. The first hamlet you reach along this part of Route 10, **North Haverhill,** is a real museum piece, with a necklace of distinctive colonial-era homes flanking an oval town green, and one of New Hampshire's oldest cemeteries close by.

Farther south spreads Loch Lyme, where the fine restaurant, rustic lodge, and cabins of **Loch Lyme Lodge** ($150 and up; 800/423-2141) have been welcoming generations of New Englanders since 1946. Swim, sail, or float out on the small lake, which has an idyllic location between the mountains and the river.

A mile south of Loch Lyme, eight miles north of Hanover, the tidy town of **Lyme** presents yet another Kodak-worthy scene, with a Soldiers and Sailors Monument standing at the center of a slender green, a large church at one end and an equally large stable at the other.

Hanover: Dartmouth College

Dartmouth College is the principal resident of attractive little **Hanover** (pop. 9,212), and the Ivy League influence shows in the local architecture, fashions, and cultural diversions. When school is in session, the cafés hum with undergraduate discourse, the downtown teems with students, and a varsity air envelops the historic campus and its sturdy neighbors. Between terms, however, the town's metabolism drops toward hibernation levels, which means there's no line for espresso.

Standing out from all the Georgian-style brick buildings is Dartmouth's **Hood Museum of Art** (closed Mon.; free; 603/646-2808), on the southeast side of the green. Housed in a modern gallery designed in part by Charles Moore, the Hood shows a changing selection from its permanent collection, but mainly hosts visiting exhibitions.

Although Ivy League Dartmouth has a $3 billion endowment and a conservative reputation, it also has had some interesting students, including children's stars **Dr. Seuss, Captain Kangaroo,** and **Mr. Rogers,** the latter two both dropouts. The poet **Robert Frost** was another famous nongraduate.

More contentious art can be experienced at the very center of Dartmouth where, in the lower level reading room of Baker Library, the walls are covered with a set of politically charged frescoes by José Clemente Orozco, *An Epic of American Civilization.*

If it's too nice a day to stay indoors and contemplate society's ills, rent a bike and ride north to Lyme and back, or borrow a canoe or kayak from Dartmouth's **Ledyard Canoe Club** ($10/hour; 603/643-6709), located on the river just north of the Route 10A bridge, and play Huck Finn for an afternoon. Or you can take a hike—the Dartmouth Outing Club maintains hundreds of miles of trails, including a part of the Appalachian Trail that runs right through town. There's an AT marker embedded in the sidewalk in front of the Hanover Inn, from where the trail runs west across the bridge to Vermont, and east down Main and Lebanon streets to the town of Etna, before climbing the 2,280-foot peak of Moose Mountain.

Hanover Practicalities

Generations of Dartmouth students have survived their college years thanks in part to the generous portions served up at **Lou's,** 30 S. Main Street (603/643-3321). Hardly changed since it opened in 1947, and famed for its magical strawberry rhubarb and other fresh-baked pies, Lou's does great big breakfasts, lunchtime soups and burgers. For dinner, head across the street to the popular **Canoe Club Bistro** (603/643-9660).

The Hanover Inn

For accommodations around Hanover, there's the stately, Dartmouth-run **Hanover Inn** facing the green ($250–350; 603/643-4300); for affordable rooms, however, look in nearby West Lebanon or across the river in White River Junction, Vermont.

Into the Mountains: Norwich, West Hartford, and Pomfret

Just uphill from where the Appalachian Trail crosses the Connecticut River, along Route 10A on a broad low bridge from Hanover, you might want to while away an afternoon in Norwich at the interesting **Montshire Museum of Science** (daily; $12; 802/649-2200), which has more than 100 educational exhibits focusing on natural history, as well as aquariums showcasing fresh- and saltwater creatures. The next town the AT passes through is West Hartford, on the banks of the White River upstream from I-91 along Route 14.

From West Hartford, you can circle around (on unnumbered and rather rough-surfaced country roads) through **North Pomfret, Pomfret,** and **South Pomfret,** passing dairy farms, quaint barns, and one post office per town, coming in through the back door to upscale Woodstock, where this AT route links up with US-4. From South Pomfret, a quaint little hamlet that's also home to the Suicide Six ski area, the hikers' Appalachian Trail heads up into the mountains through a long, roadless stretch before crossing Route 100 at Sherburne Pass. The only real driving equivalent follows Route 12 south into Woodstock.

Lebanon and West Lebanon

Sitting rather quietly a couple of miles south of Hanover, east of the Connecticut River near the point where US-4 gets submerged beneath the I-89 freeway, historic **Lebanon** (pop. 12,568) has a town green so spacious it seems more like the outskirts of a city park than the center of a town. Near the northwest corner is the main commercial area, or what's left since the malls arrived, kept alive in part by a tasty establishment: **Riverside Grill,** 65 Riverside Drive (closed in winter; 603/448-2571).

Right along the bonny banks of the Connecticut River, three miles south of patrician Hanover, the commercial busybody of **West Lebanon** has everything you probably try hard to avoid: shopping plazas, traffic tie-ups, and familiar fast *everything,* all clustered around the two local exits off the I-89 freeway.

VERMONT

Vermont is quintessential New England: picturesque villages still served by cluttered country stores, small farms nestled among the granite ridges of the Green Mountains, and needle-sharp white church spires rising above forests ablaze with autumn col-

ors. Precocious from birth—its constitution was the first in the United States to prohibit slavery and establish public schools—Vermont is known for its independent-minded politicians like Jim Jeffords and Bernie Saunders and strong liberal traditions (think Howard Dean).

From the Connecticut River, this route across Vermont follows the contours of the land, tagging along fast-running mountain streams or keeping to the valleys between the steep surrounding ridges that carry the Appalachian Trail ever southward.

White River Junction

Across the river from Hanover and Dartmouth, turn-of-the-20th-century **White River Junction** (pop. 2,582) used to echo with the sounds of some 50 trains a day traveling over six separate rail lines. The demise of the railroads and arrival of the Interstate cloverleaf on the outskirts of town effectively mothballed the downtown area, but like good vintage clothing, the photogenic historic center has been rediscovered by an art-smart crowd that doesn't mind the holes and missing buttons.

Freight trains still rumble through White River Junction a few times a day (and night!), and Amtrak stops here on its mainline Vermonter route along the Connecticut River from New York City. Apart from the trains, the main signs of life here are at breakfast and lunch, when the ancient-looking **Polka Dot Diner** (daily 5 AM–7 PM; 802/295-9722) at 7 N. Main Street serves the usual unpretentious, inexpensive grilled and fried foods. The **Tip Top Café** (802/295-3312) up the street offers delicious soups, sandwiches, and an ever-changing variety of bistro-style meals at lunch and dinner.

If you're looking for lodging with more character than the chain motels along the Interstates, consider downtown's **Hotel Coolidge** ($85 and up; 802/295-3118 or 800/622-1124) at 39 S. Main Street. In business since the 1920s, it has a nice café downstairs. It is clean, friendly, and definitely good value. Even better value are its bare-bones HI-hostel bunks and rooms, which go for around $25 per person.

Quechee and Quechee Gorge

In two miles west from White River Junction and the I-91/I-89 freeways, US-4 climbs upstream into the valley of the Ottauquechee (auto-KWEE-chee) River. You cross **Quechee Gorge** almost without warning, but adjacent parking on both sides of the gorge gives you a chance to take a longer look at the dramatic little canyon or to stretch your legs along the rimside hiking trails. East of the gorge there's a tacky Quechee Village souvenir shop, which boasts a tiny train and a well-preserved streamline-style 1946 Worcester pre-fab that's been incorporated into the **Farmers Diner** (802/295-4600), a retro all-American roadhouse serving up locally sourced versions of the usual standards.

If you're in the area around mid-June, check out the **Quechee Hot Air Balloon Festival,** held over Father's Day weekend.

Also on the east side of the gorge, **Quechee State Park** (802/295-2990) provides access to the Ottauquechee River and also has camping with hot showers. Next to the park is the nature center of the **Vermont Institute of Natural Science** (daily; $8; 802/457-2779), an outdoor museum dedicated to local wildlife, especially raptors. Enclosures let you get up close and personal with hawks, eagles, owls, and falcons.

West of the gorge, you can turn north off US-4 into old **Quechee,** a quaint town famed as the home of renowned glassblower **Simon Pearce's** lumber mill–cum–art gallery. Quechee is a fine example of how pleasant life can be once you turn away from the fast lane: a Norman Rockwell-esque rope swing hangs under a covered bridge, and on lazy summer afternoons, local youths fling them-

Quechee Gorge

selves into the river below. Join in the fun, or just soak up the ambience, with a stay (or just a memorable meal) at the **Quechee Inn,** 1119 Main Street ($120 and up; 802/295-3133), a half mile from town.

Woodstock

"The good people of Woodstock have less incentive than others to yearn for heaven," said a 19th-century resident. It's a sentiment readily echoed today. Originally settled in the 1760s, **Woodstock** (pop. 3,232) remains an exceedingly well-preserved example of small-town New England—tidy federal-

Notice, as you approach Woodstock Village Green, that there are no overhead power lines on the two main downtown streets, Central and Elm. Laurance Rockefeller paid to have the lines buried back in 1973.

style homes, built by wealthy professionals of the newborn American republic, still ring the classic village green. Now the historic village is home to wealthy retirees and their fortunate sons and daughters. You'll see the signs of this old money throughout the town: well-stocked wine racks at the general store, shady basketball courts along the river, excellent performing arts at the Town Hall Theater, and, most importantly, the wherewithal to refuse any compromising commercial development. To put it mildly, expansion of the tax base is *not* a pressing issue for this community.

During summer and fall, walking tours are an excellent way to take stock of the town's history and architecture. Call or visit the **Information Booth** (802/457-3555) on the green for a schedule. Hiking trails lead up both the summits overlooking the town. A community blackboard, a.k.a. the Town Crier, at the corner of Central and Elm, lists local events and activities all year. Even if you're racing through Woodstock, bound for the mountains, be sure to stop in Woodstock long enough to enjoy this quick tour: From the oblong green, cross the Middle Covered Bridge, and follow the Ottauquechee downstream along River Street. Then work your way back via Elm Street and **F. H. Gillingham & Sons,** Vermont's oldest country store, which offers locally made food and crafts.

Diners: Fast Food Worth Slowing Down For

Aaaah, the local diner! Throughout New England, these brightly lit establishments are magnets for folks weary of the dull predictability of the fast-food mega-chains. In contrast to the impersonal nature of those billions-serving burger factories, diners are low-key gathering spots where community gossip is shared and politics debated by a gang of regulars assembling each morning. Where motherly waitresses (frequently named Mildred, Blanche, and Edna, wearing lace hankies pinned to their aprons) are quick to offer refills on coffee. Where UPS drivers, Methodist clergy, morticians, and middle-school principals perched on adjacent stools know they can score decent hot roast-beef sandwiches or a great piece of fresh fruit pie. And where autumn leaf-peepers and other passers-through can inquire about local attractions or find out which nearby motels or B&Bs might still have empty rooms for that night.

The diner's lineage can ultimately be traced back to horse-drawn lunch carts selling sandwiches and hot coffee along the streets of cities like Providence and Boston beginning in the 1870s. However, the prototypical New England diners are those built from the 1920s through the 1950s by the Worcester Lunch Car Company: barrel-roofed with colorful porcelain panels on the exterior and plenty of varnished hardwood inside. Other diners came from manufacturers headquartered in New York (DeRaffele) and especially New Jersey (Mountain View, Fodero, Kullman, Paramount, Silk City, O'Mahony, and many more). Each diner-maker trumpeted its own design innovations: streamlined metal exteriors, artful tile work, bits of elegant stained glass, distinctive built-in clocks, and more efficient floor plans. Some even included all necessary crockery, flatware, and cooking equipment, so that new owners could begin serving hungry locals on the very day set-up was complete.

Aficionados will be quick to inform you that real

diners are roadside eateries whose component parts were fabricated in a factory, then shipped by road or rail for final assembly on-site. Real diners, they'll insist, always have counters, with at least some cooking done within view of patrons. There'll almost certainly be booths, too, and a definite blue-collar, no-frills ambience. Unlike their urban or roadside truck stop equivalents, few diners are open 24 hours; many in fact serve breakfast and lunch only, opening very early in the morning (around 6 AM) and closing around 2 or 3 PM. But not every place with the word "diner" in its name is the genuine article. Many places that call themselves diners are as far removed from the classic prefab as IKEA furniture is from a handcrafted antique, and mavens regard diner-themed restaurants (like the current generation of Johnny Rockets) with considerable scorn. The smaller, the better, they say, with points deducted for any remodeling that disfigures the original design.

You needn't care about any of this lore, of course, to enjoy yourself. But after visiting your third or fourth diner, you may begin to notice similarities and differences among them. Curious about a particular establishment's history? Quiz the owner—more often than not, he or she will be happy to tell you all about the place, which may have started life with a different name in another town and been moved three or more times before it found its current home. Look for a "tag," the small metal plate (often affixed to the wall over the entry door) listing manufacturer, date, and serial number. The best and most enjoyable way to get to know diners and diner culture is simply to spend time in them, but if you want to learn more, check the authoritative volume, *American Diner Then and Now* by Richard Gutman, published by Johns Hopkins University Press.

If you've admired the rolling fields and weathered wooden fences, savored the local apples and sharp cheddar, and enjoyed the scent of mown hay or boiling maple sap, you'll appreciate an even closer look at New England's farms with a visit to the **Billings Farm & Museum** (daily in summer, weekends the rest of the year; $11; 802/457-2355), on Route 12 north of the village. Frederick Billings, better known as the builder of the Northern Pacific Railroad (Billings, Montana is named for him), began this working dairy farm in the late 19th century. Its restored farmhouse and huge barns illustrate the rural life in galleries, demonstrations, and hands-on activities.

Across the road, another historic farm is open to the public as the **Marsh-Billings-Rockefeller National Historical Park** (tours daily; $8; 802/457-3368), Vermont's only national park. The property, which includes the former home of Laurance Rockefeller (1910-2004), who married Frederick Billings's granddaughter, is a study in conservation practice, and its dense woodlands are living proof of the merits of sustainable agriculture.

Woodstock Practicalities

Hungry travelers will find plenty of choices around town. There are also two very interesting if rather bare-bones road-food haunts bookending the town along US-4. At the east end of town, you'll find the white shack housing **WASP's Snack Bar,** 57 Pleasant Street (802/457-9805). On US-4 a half mile west of the

green at 462 Woodstock Road is the open-air (which in Vermont means summer-only) **White Cottage Snack Bar** (802/457-3455), serving up ace burgers and deep-friend clams. Next to the White Cottage is a healthier alternative, the **Woodstock Farmer's Market** (802/457-3658), with top-quality produce and deli fare.

Accommodations run the gamut from moderate motels to deluxe inns; at all of them, expect rates to increase during high season, which in Woodstock is most of summer and fall, along with the winter holidays. The main place right in town, the 144-room, Rockefeller-built **Woodstock Inn** ($250 and up; 802/457-1100) sits on the south side of the green, and although it tries hard to look like a stately old place, the inn was actually built from scratch in 1969. The **Village Inn** (802/457-1255), a lovely Victorian-era B&B at 41 Pleasant Street, has much more character, yet is still affordable. The modest **Braeside Motel** ($70 and up; 802/457-1366), along US-4 on the eastern outskirts of town, is about as budget-friendly as you're going to get.

Bridgewater and Killington

The tiny town of **Bridgewater** (pop. 895), stretching along the banks of the Ottauquechee, seems well on the way to the middle of nowhere. But that's what lures many visitors to this region—the fact that so much of it seems to have contentedly hung back with Rip van Winkle. That said, Bridgewater *is* a gateway to one of the state's most important somewheres: the ski resorts of central Vermont. The large woolen mill here has been converted into the Old Mill Marketplace, its water-powered turbines and textile machines replaced by small shops selling a typically Vermont mix of antiques, ski apparel, New Age books, and gift-packaged Vermont foods to visitors heading for the mountains.

Through the Bridgewater area, US-4 is generously wide-shouldered and level, making it a popular cycling route, especially during the fall color season, when the dense hardwood forests that climb the slopes above the roadway are blazing with autumn hues. When the leaves have fallen and been replaced by snow, this scenic stretch changes character completely, becoming one of the East Coast's most prominent ski resorts, **Killington.** The permanent population of Killington is maybe 50 people, but on winter weekends as many as 10,000 skiers flock to its seven different mountains and many

Vermont holds more than 100 covered bridges, several good examples of which are to be seen between Quechee and Bridgewater. Look for the 1836 **Taftsville Bridge** west of Quechee, the **Middle Bridge** in Woodstock (which was totally rebuilt way back in 1969), and the 1877 **Lincoln Bridge** four miles west of Woodstock. The nation's longest covered bridge crosses the Connecticut River at Windsor, about 15 miles southeast of Woodstock, with a 460-foot span built in 1866.

In the Killington area, tune to **"The Peak,"** WEBK **105.3 FM,** for the best in alternative pop music—everything from the Grateful Dead to Beck and Bela Fleck.

miles of trails (lift tickets around $80; snow info 800/621-6867). The skiers also support a plethora of real estate agencies, restaurants, and bars, especially off US-4 on the main road to the slopes, Killington Road.

Compared to the rest of Vermont, Killington is not an especially attractive place to be in summer, when the parking lots of the time-share condo complexes are empty and the hills are scarred by clear-cut ski trails, but the lack of crowds also means lower prices for accommodations. Everywhere from roadside motels to upscale resorts like the **Inn at Six Mountains** offer their lowest rates when the temperatures are highest.

Gifford Woods State Park

Sitting in the scenic heart of the Green Mountains, at the junction of US-4 and Route 100, **Gifford Woods State Park** (802/775-5354) protects one of the few virgin forests left in New England, with seven acres of massive sugar maple, birch, and ash trees, some of which are more than 300 years old. There's a nice **campground** with hot showers, and access to many fine trails, including the Appalachian Trail and the Long Trail, which run together across US-4 just west of 2,190-foot Shelburne Pass.

Route 100: Rochester, Hancock, and Granville Gulf

Route 100 runs north–south through the geographical and spiritual heart of Vermont, winding from curve to curve past cornfields and fat cows lazing in impossibly green pastures, alongside gurgling streams, up and down switchbacking passes, and generally setting the standard for what scenic roads ought to be. Route 100 runs right at the edge of the Green Mountains National Forest, parallel to Vermont's beloved crestline Long Trail, and every so often passes by a picturesque gas station–cum–general store, selling everything you'll need to keep you on the road, from gas to maple-syrup milk shakes. Up and down the whole state of Vermont, Route 100 is a wonderful drive, as are just about all of the roads that intersect it.

North of US-4, the first place you come to along Route 100 is **Pittsfield,** an all-in-white hamlet set in a pastoral valley and surrounded by hayfields and acres of corn. From here Route 100 edges east into the White River Valley, passing through

Stockbridge, which centers on an ancient-looking Ford dealership, and a couple more places that seem to exist solely on maps. The next stop is **Rochester,** at the junction with Route 73, which heads west over scenic Brandon Gap. Rochester is a proper Vermont town, with a village green, a bandstand, and the excellent **Rochester Café** (802/767-4302), serving breakfast and lunch (and bread pudding and milk shakes—yum).

Two miles south of Rochester, across the river and away from Route 100, the **Liberty Hill Farm B&B** ($90 per person; 802/767-3926) is a family-friendly farmstay B&B and has a working 100-plus-acre dairy where you can hike, bike, fish, or help feed the cows (and the ducks and chickens and cats).

North of Rochester, Route 100 passes through a still-working landscape, with ski club cabins sharing the roadside scene with a few barns and remnants of historic sheep pens. The one don't-miss highlight of this middle section of Route 100 is **Granville Gulf State Preserve,** about 30 beautiful miles north from US-4. The Green Mountains rise steeply to either side of the road, and just off the west side of the road, delicate **Moss Glen Falls** tumble down through craggy cliffs to a gurgling stream. A short boardwalk, built using recycled wood products and supermarket plastic bags, leads to the foot of the falls from a small parking turnout.

Plymouth and Plymouth Notch: Calvin Coolidge Country

Running a twisty seven miles south from US-4 and Bridgewater, Route 100A passes through beautiful scenery and **Plymouth Notch,** birthplace of Calvin Coolidge, the only U.S. president born on the 4th of July. The small hilltop clutch of buildings is so little changed by modern times, it's a

"Silent Cal" Coolidge

"Silent Cal" Coolidge was famous—perhaps unjustly—for being a man of few words. A White House dinner guest is said to have bet that she could make the president address her with at least three words; when confronted with this challenge, Coolidge replied, "You lose."

wonder there aren't horses with carriages parked behind the visitors center instead of Subarus. One of the most evocative and simply beautiful historic sites in New England, the **Coolidge homestead** has been restored to its 1923 appearance, the year Colonel John Coolidge administered the oath of office to his vacationing son, the vice president, after President Harding died unexpectedly in San Francisco. The house, the general store, and the cheese factory are three of the 10 buildings open to the public (daily in summer; $7.50; 802/672-3773). There's also a mile-long nature trail offering fine views of Plymouth Notch and its Green Mountain surroundings.

Route 100: The Skiers' Highway

Known as the Skiers' Highway, serpentine Route 100 manages to pass the base of nearly every major ski resort in southern Vermont. From Ludlow south through Jamaica, Stratton, and West Dover, any doubt that skiing is the cash cow of the state's most lucrative industry—tourism—is quickly dispelled by the wall-to-wall inns, sportswear shops, vacation real estate offices, and restaurants along the way.

In recent years, downhill mountain-bikers and inn-to-inn cyclists riding Route 100 have made the region more of a year-round recreation center, but overall you still get the sense that, pretty as they are with their village greens, old homes, and hand-carved wooden signs, many of these Route 100 towns spend the warm months convalescing.

Brigham Young, the man who led the Mormon exodus to Utah, was born in **Whitingham,** fewer than 10 miles south of Wilmington on Route 100, at the south end of the Harriman Reservoir. There's a small commemorative monument and picnic area on the Town Hall Common.

Wilmington and Route 9

Route 100 catches a panoramic view of Mt. Snow as the roadway descends into **Wilmington** (pop. 1,968), a picturesque village of 18th- and 19th-century shops and houses built along the Deerfield River. Wilmington also has some great old-fashioned places to eat like **Dot's Restaurant,** 3 W. Main Street (802/464-7284), a white-clapboard Vermont institution, famous for its pancakes, burgers, chili, and pies. The chamber of commerce is named after the local Mount Snow ski resort rather than the town, so you know who pays the bills around here. Nevertheless, the warmer months see a fair bit of activity in the galleries and antique shops, and for classical music lovers, the **Marlboro Music Festival** (802/254-2394 in summer only) marks summer's zenith at Marlboro College, a dozen miles east toward Brattleboro on Route 9. Between mid-July and mid-August several score of the world's finest classical musicians perform here in one of the nation's most distinguished annual chamber music series.

> Whether or not you need gas, those interested in old cars and automobilia will want to stop by the full-service, re-created Sunoco filling station and antique car collection at **Hemmings Motor News** (800/227-4373), at 215 Main Street in Bennington.

Heading westward toward Bennington, you can continue west on Route 9 to Bennington and follow US-7 south through Williamstown, or you can make your way south through the much less developed areas along Route 8 and Route 100, which take you through the heavy-duty mill town of North Adams.

Bennington

By far the largest Vermont town south of Burlington, **Bennington** (pop. 16,451) is a bustling little manufacturing and commercial center. It was the site of a significant victory against the British-paid Hessians in 1777 during the American Revolution, a sweet morale-booster that contributed to the defeat of General "Gentleman Johnny" Burgoyne's army of Redcoats at Saratoga. In the subsequent centuries, Bennington's name became synonymous with art: the decorative arts of the antebellum United States Pottery Company; the liberal arts of **Bennington College,** one of the nation's most expensive and exclusive private colleges; and the folk art of Mary Robertson "Grandma" Moses.

The largest public collection of Grandma Moses's beguiling work is on display in the **Bennington Museum** (closed Wed.; $9), whose ivy-covered edifice is found up the hill at

When garnished with Vermont-made **Ben & Jerry's** ice cream, apple pie à la mode is certainly nothing to sneer at, but if you really want to try apple pie the Vermont way, ask for a slab of sharp cheddar on the side instead of ice cream.

75 West Main Street (Route 9) in the graceful old part of town. Along with 30 Grandma Moses paintings and the rural schoolhouse she attended two centuries ago, the museum also has a wide variety of historical artifacts, examples of early Bennington pottery, and the sole survivor of the fabulous motor cars once made here in Bennington: a 1925 Wasp.

From the Bennington Museum, walk north toward the 306-foot obelisk that towers over the town: the **Bennington Battle Monument,** erected in 1891 to commemorate the Revolutionary War victory, which actually occurred west of

town, over the New York state border. For $2, mid-April–November 1, an elevator will take you to an observation room near the top of the tower for a great view up and down the valley.

Bennington is also the final resting place of poet Robert Frost, whose tombstone in the burial ground alongside the Old First Church, at Church and Monument Streets, says: "I had a lover's quarrel with the world."

If anyone starts erecting monuments to good dining instead of old wars or dead poets, this town would have another tower of stone beside the **Blue Benn Diner** (802/442-5140), on a bend in US-7 north of town at 314 North Street. The fact that it's a vintage 1940s Silk City certainly gives this cozy, nonsmoking joint character. But what earns the seven-days-a-week (from 6 AM) loyalty of its patrons is the top-notch short-order cooking: From baked meat loaf and roast pork to broccoli stir-fry and multigrain pancakes, the food's good, cheap, and served up so fast you'll barely have time to choose your song on the wall-hung jukebox at your table.

Most of Bennington's accommodations are strung along Route 7A to the north and US-7 to the south of downtown, all local names but for the Ramada and Best Western inns found on 7A. If you are in the market for a distinctive B&B, check out the central, historic, and highly regarded **Four Chimneys Inn** ($135 and up; 802/447-3500), which offers 11 rooms and 11 acres of grounds and gardens, and a fine restaurant, west of Bennington on Route 9 at 21 West Road.

MASSACHUSETTS

Hemmed in by the daunting to-pography of its surrounding mountains, the Berkshire region of western Massachusetts is a world apart, blessed with abundant nature and an easygoing small-town character. The region's relaxed, rural charms and its location equidistant from Boston and New York City have long made it a magnet for writers and artists as well as a playground for the rich, so be prepared to experience a little of everything from natural splendors to high-society display. And remember, it never takes more than a few strategic turns to trade plush restaurants and music festivals for splendidly rural forests as deep and undisturbed as any in New England.

North Adams

If you've grown accustomed to the typical tourist New England of village greens and clapboard B&Bs, industrial **North Adams** (pop. 14,681) may come as something of a shock. Nearly from its inception, North Adams tied its fortunes to major manufacturing plants, churning out printed cotton until textiles went south, then rolling out electronics for everything from the first atomic bomb to the television sets of the 1950s and 1960s. When electronics went solid-state and overseas, North Adams nearly died clinging to the belief that some new assembly line would come fill its sprawling complex of massive Victorian-era mill buildings. Finally, the town's long-awaited salvation seems to be taking shape, in the form of art: the Massachusetts Museum of Contemporary Art. Better known as **Mass MoCA** (daily in July & Aug., closed Tues. rest of year; $15; 413/662-2111), the museum galleries fill some 200,000 square feet of heavy-duty

By the early 19th century, farmland had replaced 75 percent of Berkshire County's forests. Now forests have reclaimed that 75 percent and more, but innumerable dry stone walls serve as reminders of the once vast cultivated fields.

North Adams is five miles north of the quaint town of **Adams,** the birthplace of voting rights activist Susan B. Anthony (1820–1906).

industrial buildings with an ever-changing array of cutting-edge art plus the inevitable gift shop, a very nice café, frequent live music, and even its own very stylish B&B, **Porches,** at 231 River Street ($175 and up; 413/664-0400).

For those more interested in the olden days, the region's historic gravy train is faithfully recollected in the **Western Gateway Heritage State Park** (daily; free; 413/663-6312). Occupying the former freight yard of the Boston and Maine Railroad, the park highlights the landmark construction of the five-mile-long Hoosac Tunnel and North Adams's front-row seat on the Boston–Great Lakes rail connection it made possible.

Williamstown

To the visitor it appears as if stately **Williamstown** (pop. 4,754) is simply a nickname for the immaculate and graceful campus of Williams College—even the main commercial block is basically the corridor between dorms and gym. From their common 18th-century benefactor, Ephraim Williams (who insisted the town's name be changed from its original West Hoosuck), to the large number of alumni who return in their retirement, "Billsville" and its college are nearly insepa-rable. The town-gown symbiosis has spawned an enviable array of visual, performing, and edible arts, yet fresh contin-gents of ingenuous youth keep all the wealth and refinement from becoming too cloying.

Singer Sewing Machine heir Robert Sterling Clark's huge art collection ended up in Williamstown in part because of the Cold War. In the late 1940s and early 1950s, the threat of a Russian nuclear attack seemed real enough that being as distant as possible from likely bomb targets was a critical fac-tor in choosing a permanent repository. Today **Clark Art Institute** (daily July and Aug., closed Mon. Sept.–June; $12.50 in summer, free rest of year; 413/458-2303), at 225 South Street, is the town's jewel, displaying paintings by Winslow Homer and an extraordinary collection of Impressionist works, including more than 30 Renoirs. Also worth a look is the excellent and wide-ranging **Williams College Museum of Art** (closed Mon.; free; 413/597-2429) on Main Street opposite Memorial Chapel (that mini Westminster Abbey).

Williamstown can claim another gem, this time in the nat-ural art of relaxation. Luxurious Cunard Lines used to serve its ocean-going passengers water exclusively from Williamstown's **Sand Springs** (Memorial Day–Labor Day; $7.50; 413/458-5205). Since the 1950s, a family-friendly swimming pool complex has opened on the site, on the north side of town at 158 Sand Springs Road, all summer long.

> It was during the blasting of the **Hoosac Tunnel** that nitroglycerin was first used as a construction explosive. And just so you know, the river is the Hoosic, but the mountain range is the Hoosac.

Williamstown Practicalities

For breakfast, head to US-7 on the north side of town, where the popular **Chef's Hat** (413/458-5120) at 905 Simonds Road preserves a 100-year-old counter and other parts of its original diner incarnation. Also good, the **Clarksburg Bread Company** (closed Sun. and Mon.; 413/458-2251) at 37 Spring Street serves up soups, sandwiches, and a wealth of delicious baked goods until 4 PM The hands-down best takeout pizza joint is **Hot Tomatoes** (413/458-2722), at 100 Water Street, and in mild weather the nearby streamside park is well suited to lolling picnickers.

Tony continental dining suitable for starched alumni banquets abounds in Williamstown, but if you're looking for truly fresh, interesting food, skip the inns and go to **Mezze** (413/458-0123) at 16 Water Street, where the very best locally sourced produce, meats and fish are featured on a stylish, dinner-only menu.

A drive along Main Street (Route 2) will give you a view of most of Williamstown's accommodations, including many small motels out on the eastern edge of town like the friendly and clean **Maple Terrace** at 555 Main Street ($75 and up; 413/458-9677). For a real treat, consider **Field Farm** ($125 and up;

Hancock Shaker Village

Just five miles west of Pittsfield on old US-20, Hancock Shaker Village is one of the best-preserved remnants of the religious sect known popularly as Shakers, but formally as the United Society of Believers in Christ's Second Appearing, whose utopian communities flourished in the years before the Civil War. Shakers, as outsiders called them because of their occasional convulsions during worship, were dedicated to a communal life conspicuous in its equality between men and women, a natural corollary to their belief in parity between a male God and a female Holy Mother Wisdom.

The English-born leader of the group, Ann Lee, was in fact regarded by Shakers as the female, and second, incarnation of Christ. Although Puritan theocracy was ending, preaching this gospel did not endear her to many New Englanders in the decade following her arrival just prior to the American Revolution. During that war, Lee and her "children" sought their Heaven on Earth, as seen in her visions. Mother Ann died near Albany, New York, in 1784, before any communities based on her precepts could be founded.

Hancock Shaker Village, third among the 24 settlements built in the nation by Lee's followers, was found-

413/458-3135) at 554 Sloan Road in South Williamstown, five miles south along either Route 7 or scenic Water Street (Route 43). Occupying the 254-acre former estate of Pacific Northwest lumber tycoon Lawrence Bloedel, the main house, designed in 1948, is a striking example of American mid-century modern architecture. If you have any love of Frank Lloyd Wright or Charles and Ray Eames, you'll be delighted by this live-in museum of contemporary design, with its huge picture windows, proto-Scandinavian furniture, and meadowside swimming pool.

Mt. Greylock

South of Williamstown, Massachusetts' tallest peak is the centerpiece of 12,500-acre **Mount Greylock State Reservation,** one of the state's largest and most popular possessions. More than 50 miles of trails, including some thigh-burning mountain-ed in 1790 and survived 170 years, outlasting all but two other Shaker communities. It's been preserved as a living museum (daily Apr.–Oct.; $15; 413/443-0188 or 800/817-1137), with exhibits, tours, and working artisans interpreting the rural lifestyle and famous design skills of the Shakers.

Appreciation of the efficiency, simplicity, and perfect workmanship consecrated within the "City of Peace" can quickly fill a couple of days if you let it. For a special treat, secure a place at the candlelight Shaker dinners held on Saturday evenings; you can also sample Shaker cuisine in the Village Cafe.

The center of Shaker activities was just west of Hancock, along US-20 across the New York border at New Lebanon, where a few buildings still stand today. Other large Shaker communities in New England included Sabbathday Lake in Maine (the only one still "alive"), one at Enfield, New Hampshire (east of Hanover), and another at Canterbury, New Hampshire (south of Franconia Notch).

bike routes, wander along the reforested slopes, most of which were heavily logged for fuel and pulp back in the 19th century. Rock ledges provide great views of the Hoosic River Valley to the east and the Housatonic Valley to the south, when the namesake mists aren't keeping the 3,491-foot summit wadded up in a damp ball of dingy cotton. The $25 million reconstruction project has been a complete success, and during warm months, access is a cinch: Century-old Notch Road snakes its way up through the birch and spruce from Route 2 on the north side, while Rockwell Road ascends more gently from US-7 along the flanks of Greylock's

southern neighbors. Combine these roads' 17 miles and you'll enjoy the most scenic, driveable mountain ascent in New England, although keep in mind that both roads are narrow, enlivened by occasional hairpin turns, and—especially at dusk—prone to wandering wildlife.

If you want to see over the forest, climb the 105-foot **War Memorial Tower** on the summit. If the weather is good, you'll have a panoramic view from New Hampshire to Connecticut. A stone's throw from the granite tower is the **Bascom Lodge** ($35 per person; 413/743-1591) a beautiful old stone and timber structure that offers private rooms ($100), shared bunk rooms, and showers.

Pittsfield

Compared to the carefully preserved Norman Rockwell simplicity of many of the surrounding small towns, the aging industrial cityscape of **Pittsfield** (pop. 45,793) has made it the place most Berkshire weekenders strenuously try to avoid, despite the fact that its size and the valley's topography make this nearly impossible unless you have a resident's familiarity with the back roads.

Despite Pittsfield's anything-but-quaint appearance, there are actually some good reasons to pay the place a visit. Head out to Holmes Road, at the city's rural southern edge, and maybe you will see the resemblance between a leviathan and the imposing outline of Mt. Greylock, particularly if you view it from the study window of Herman Melville's **Arrowhead** (daily in summer; $12; 413/442-1793). That salty masterpiece, *Moby Dick,* was indeed written in this landlocked locale, where Melville moved in 1850 to be near his mentor,

Arrowhead

Nathaniel Hawthorne. While foremost a literary shrine, the spacious farm is also home to the **Berkshire County Historical Society,** whose well-curated exhibits are always interesting. Serious pilgrims on the path of Ishmael and the great white whale will also want to visit the Melville Memorial Room on the upper level of the **Berkshire Athenaeum,** Pittsfield's public library, at 1 Wendell Avenue.

As with its other attractions, Pittsfield has some real unexpected gems when it comes to food. For excellent pasta, pizza, and pub grub at a great small-town price, cruise over to the **East Side Cafe** (413/447-9405), at 378 Newell Street, a neighborhood bar whose comfort food and convivial atmosphere attract a family clientele.

Lenox: Tanglewood and The Mount

During the late-19th-century Gilded Age, the Berkshires were the inland equivalent of Newport, Rhode Island, with dozens of opulent "cottages" constructed here by newly rich titans of American industry. Built for an era in which "society" was a respectable, full-time occupation for folks with names like Carnegie and Westinghouse, some 75 of these giant mansions still stand, especially around the genteel town of **Lenox** (pop. 5,100). Many of the houses have been converted to palatial B&B inns, full-service health spas, or private schools; others are home to organizations whose presence has made Lenox a seasonal mecca for the performing arts.

The lives and times of the Gilded Age elite were well chronicled by Edith Wharton, who lived in Lenox for many years in a 42-room house she designed and built for herself called **The Mount** (daily in summer only; $16; 413/551-5122). Recently restored and set in three acres of Italianate gardens, The Mount is just south of central Lenox, well signed off Plunkett Street. Wharton, who considered herself better at gardening than writing, was the first woman to win a Pulitzer Prize (for her 1920 novel *The Age of Innocence*). She drew upon local people and incidents in many of her works, including two of her most famous: *The House of Mirth* and *Ethan Frome.*

Lenox is also connected with another great American writer, Nathaniel Hawthorne, who lived here with his family around 1850 and wrote *The House of Seven Gables* at what is now the summer home of the Boston Symphony and many visiting performers, **Tanglewood** (tickets $20 and up; 888/266-2100). Besides Tanglewood, the Lenox area also hosts the Jacob's Pillow dance festival in Becket (413/243-0745) and the Berkshire Theatre Festival in Stockbridge (413/298-5536), so you can understand why such a small town is such a big magnet for East Coast culture vultures.

Lenox Practicalities

The Berkshires' annual influx of cosmopolitan concert-goers affects everything in southwestern Massachusetts, most obviously the local restaurants, half of which cater to seasonal immigrants from Boston and New York. Try the eclectic (and not too expensive) menu at the tiny, unpretentious **Dish Café,** 37 Church Street (413/637-1800), where the tastes from the kitchen highlight taste sensations from all over the map. Many other contenders for the town's gourmet dining crown lie within the same two-block area.

Along with its many good restaurants, Lenox brims with more than 20 handsome B&B inns, all attractively situated amid wide lawns and gardens. Try the historic **Birchwood Inn** ($125 and up; 413/637-2600), at 7 Hubbard Street, opposite the Church on the Hill; or the **Brook Farm Inn** ($150 and up; 413/637-3013) at 15 Hawthorne Street, which offers more than 700 volumes of poetry in the library, poetry on audiotape, poetry readings on Saturday, and poems *du jour* for perusal before breakfast. Another popular option, right at the center of Lenox, is the always charming **Village Inn,** 16 Church Street ($125 and up; 413/637-0020), built in 1771 and featuring clean, comfortable rooms and a very good restaurant.

Stockbridge

On the south side of the I-90 Mass Turnpike from Lenox, the other main center of Berkshires cultural life is **Stockbridge** (pop. 2,276). If Main Street feels familiar, perhaps it's because the town made its way onto Norman Rockwell canvases during the final decades of his career, when he lived and worked here. You may dismiss his illustrations as the epitome of contrived sentimentality, but only people with hearts of solid flint won't find themselves grinning after a stroll through the collection of the **Norman Rockwell Museum** (daily; $15; 413/298-4100). The modern museum is on Route 183 two miles west of town, and the town itself is well worth a stroll, too, particularly past the grand houses along Main Street that seem frozen in an idyllic past.

Stockbridge's Main Street hasn't always been the exclusive province of boutiques for coffee, curtains, and AARP members. Once upon a time it was also home to the eatery immortalized by **Arlo Guthrie** as the place where "you can get anything you want" in his 1967 folk song, "Alice's Restaurant Massacree."

While most of the large estate homes

around Stockbridge are not open to the public, one of the county's more extravagant "cottages" is **Naumkeag** (daily in summer only; $12), an 1885 mansion on Prospect Hill Road less than a mile north of downtown. The mansion, designed by Stanford White for Joseph Choate, a lawyer who later served as U.S. ambassador to Britain, amply illustrates why this region was regarded as the state's Gold Coast a century ago. The impressively landscaped grounds are an attraction in their own right.

Know that **Rockwell** painting of the runaway kid with the policeman? The lunch-counter setting was inspired by **Joe's Diner** (413/243-9756) at 85 Center Street in nearby Lee, a Berkshire institution favored by everybody from local factory workers to New York celebrities.

Sculpture is the highlight of **Chesterwood** (daily in summer; $15), off Route 183 just south of the Rockwell Museum. The residence was the summer home of Daniel Chester French, one of the most popular contributors to the fin-de-siècle American renaissance. French arrived on the art scene with a bang, sculpting Concord's *Minute Man* statue at age 25, but he is best remembered for his statue of the seated president in Lincoln Memorial in Washington, D.C. A tour of French's studio and house (now a property of the National Trust) or a walk around the 122 wooded acres graced with works of contemporary sculptors quickly confirms why French once called his seasonal visits "six months…in heaven."

Tyringam

Route 8, US-20, and the Mass Turnpike all cross the Appalachian Trail at Greenwater Pond east of Lee, but a much more scenic stretch of the trail can be accessed south of here in the village of **Tyringham** (pop. 370). Site of a Shaker community in the 1800s, and later a popular artist colony, this small hamlet is situated in a delightfully rural landscape of small farms and rolling pastures. The main sight here is an odd one: **Santarella** (daily; $4), the hand-hewn home and studio of British sculptor Sir Henry Kitson, whose many works include the Pilgrim monument at Plymouth and the *Minute Man* at Lexington Green. His house is a place where Bilbo Baggins of

The Hobbit would feel at home, with its sculpted rocks, twisting beams, and organic-looking pseudo-thatched roof.

South of Santarella, beyond the ever-quaint center of Tyringham, a signed parking area marks the crossing of the Appalachian Trail, which you can follow on a short (three-mile round-trip) hike through fields of wildflowers up through Tyringham Cobble to a ridge giving a good view over this pastoral valley, which feels far more remote than it really is.

Great Barrington

The first black man ever to earn a Ph.D. from Harvard, writer **W. E. B. DuBois,** was born in Great Barrington in 1868.

When people think of electricity they think of Thomas Edison and light bulbs, but the roots of your local utility lie here in the nation's first commercial electrical system, created by transformer inventor **William Stanley** for Great Barrington's downtown in 1886.

The mountainous section of US-20, north of the Mass Turnpike between Huntington and Lee, is one of the oldest auto roads in New England, originally called **Jacob's Ladder.** Older, and in some ways prettier, than the busier and much more famous Mohawk Trail across the state's northwestern tier, Jacob's Ladder is centered on the quaint town of **Chester.**

While most South County towns have been spruced up like precious antiques, **Great Barrington,** with as many hardware stores as chic boutiques, is like grandma's comfortable old sofa, still too much in daily use to keep under velvet wraps. The town doesn't deplore the few tacky commercial lots around its fringes, perhaps because they can't detract from the handsome buildings at its core. Prime among these buildings, which include stone churches on wide Main Street and imposing Searles Castle, a former Berkshire cottage turned private academy, is the landmark **Mahaiwe Theater** (413/528-0100) at 14 Castle Street, all marble and gilt trim behind its marquee. Built for vaudeville and recently restored, the Mahaiwe still hosts frequent films, theater, and musical theater productions.

Besides architecture and history, Great Barrington has a lot to offer hungry travelers. Fussy early-risers seeking their cappuccino and muffins, or picnickers needing the makings of a great spread will want to check out **Uncommon Grounds,** 403 Stockbridge Road (US-7), which serves up espresso drinks, teas, and bakery items, with the added benefit of the South County's best let's-hang-out atmosphere. **Bev's Homemade Ice Cream,** down the street at 5 Railroad Street, is another source of caffeine, light lunch fare, and sugar, by the rich and creamy coneful.

Sheffield: Bartholomew's Cobble

Between Great Barrington and the Connecticut state line, US-7 winds through **Sheffield** and is lined by dozens of antique stores, earning this stretch the nickname "Antique Alley." Sheffield also has a faded gray covered bridge, just 100 yards east of US-7 on the north side of town. At the south edge of Sheffield, just west of US-7 off Weatogue Road, the natural rock garden of **Bartholomew's Cobble** rises up above the west bank of the Housatonic River. Geology and

The last battle of **Shay's Rebellion,** an uprising of farmers demanding reforms to prevent foreclosures after the American Revolution dried up English credit, was fought in a field south of the village on Sheffield Road. A small stone obelisk marks the spot, coincidentally adjacent to the Appalachian Trail.

weather have conspired to produce an outstanding diversity of plants and birds—more than 700 species, including beautiful wildflowers—within a relatively small pocket of fern-covered limestone outcrops and broad meadows. At the center of the 300-acre state-run reserve ($5), a very pleasant walk up Hulburt's Hill gives a broad view over the surrounding Berkshire scene.

South Egremont: Bash Bish Falls

While US-7 gets the most tourist traffic, a more pastoral way south into Connecticut follows Route 41 via **South Egremont,** another of those well-preserved villages entirely ensconced in the National Register of Historic Places, which is hardly a rare honor in Massachusetts. At the center of town, **Mom's Country Café,** 65 Main Street (413/528-2414), is a friendly choice for a bite before or after a hike; you'll find country breakfasts, burgers, pasta, and soups.

Bash Bish Falls

South Egremont is the gateway to the state's remotest corner, the

4,000 forested acres of Mount Washington State Forest. Within its wooded boundaries are miles of hiking trails, including a stretch of the Appalachian Trail climbing up to the 2,602-foot summit of Mt. Everett, but the highlight here is photogenic **Bash Bish Falls,** the highest in Massachusetts. A whopping 80-foot drop, splashing down in a V-shaped pair of cascades, Bash Bish Falls is no Niagara, but it's a nice place to while away a hot summer afternoon.

CONNECTICUT

Anyone who drives its Interstates will appreciate why Connecticut enjoys a solid reputation among New Englanders as "the drive-through state." The high-speed route between Boston and New York City, I-95, is something endured rather than enjoyed, but our route through the scenic northwest corner is as different from the coastal megalopolis as a tulip is from a truck tire. Like the neighboring Berkshires, Connecticut's Litchfield Hills are a traditional retreat for discerning city dwellers. The area is rich in forests, farms, and picturesque little towns laden with antiques and great restaurants. Fast food and discount shopping are as alien to this landscape as affordability, so if your purse strings are tight you'll want to keep moving; otherwise, linger a while and enjoy some of the rural charm so prized by those people you might see on the cover of *Business Week*.

North Canaan and Salisbury

Crossing into Connecticut from the north on US-7, the first thing that will catch your eye is the stainless-steel siding of **Collin's Diner** at 100 W. Main Street (860/824-7040) in the heart of **North Canaan**. A classic 1940s prefab O'Mahony diner, Collin's has all the usual diner standards, and its big parking lot (shared with the neighboring historic railroad depot) is frequently full of equally classic cars, whose owners congregate here on summer afternoons. The rest of North Canaan—a couple of clothing stores and an old movie theater—is anything but prissy, a refreshing change of pace from the overly tidy tourist towns that dominate the surrounding region.

Collin's Diner in North Canaan

From North Canaan, US-44 winds east toward Hartford, stopping after 15 miles at another gem of a small town, **Norfolk;** if any town has capitalized on being far removed from trading floors and board meetings, it's this one. With three public parks and the largest private forest in the state, Norfolk has considered its sheer scenic beauty a stock in trade for nearly a century; the town green is worth the drive, so you can see the folksy road sign that points the way with pictures of rabbits and other cute creatures.

> Salisbury's **Lakeville Furnace** was the armory of the American Revolution, supplying George Washington's troops with almost their entire arsenal of artillery and ammunition for the duration of the war.

After extensive touring around New England, you risk taking white columns, wide porches, picket fences, and the obligatory Congregational steeple for granted. Even then, prim little **Salisbury,** a half dozen miles west of US-7 at the junction of Route 41 and US-44, still may elicit reveries about what small-town America would look like if strip malls ceased to exist. Spend an afternoon sipping cardamom-scented tea in

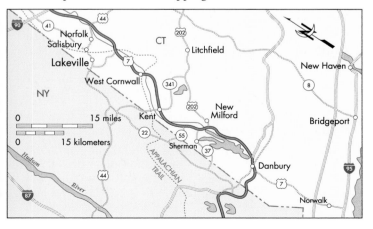

tiny **Chaiwalla,** on US-44 at 1 Main Street (860/435-9758), and see if you disagree that franchising of food and drink should be declared a misdemeanor.

West Cornwall

Rivers are consistently some of the most attractive driving companions you could ask for, a fact proven once again as US-7 rejoins the Housatonic River south of Lime Rock. The highway's scenic miles are further enhanced by the sudden appearance of a barn-red covered bridge, which since 1837 has served as the one-lane gateway to idyllic **West Cornwall.** This is the kind of place that would tar and feather the first vinyl-siding salesperson to walk into town, lest harm befall its antiquarian bookshop or other clapboard buildings bearing signs from previous commercial lives.

LIME ROCK PARK

On Route 112 a couple of miles west of US-7, you'll find **Lime Rock Park,** an automobile racetrack made famous in part by classic car rallies, a mid-May Grand Prix, the Skip Barber Racing School, and the occasional appearance of celebrity drivers. The sharp, twisting descent from nearby Lakeville to the raceway is one of many pretty back-road drives in the area.

South of town, **Housatonic Meadows State Park** (860/672-6772) offers riverside camping, perfectly situated for anyone considering a canoe or kayak rental from adjacent **Clarke Outdoors,** on US-7 a mile south of that covered bridge. Clarke's 10-mile canoe trips (around $50 for 2 people; 860/672-6365) include a boat, life-vests and all the gear, plus van shuttles and hot showers. Remember to bring bug repellent if you're planning to spend time near the water.

Housatonic Meadows State Park also includes a short, three-mile round-trip trail up 1,160-foot Pine Knob, which offers fine views from its summit. Just south of the park boundary, the hikers' Appalachian Trail crosses US-7 and the Housatonic River at the hamlet of Cornwall Bridge, then runs alongside the river for some eight miles, the longest riverside cruise in the trail's entire 2,100 miles.

Kent

Like many of its Litchfield-area neighbors, **Kent** (pop. 2,918) had a thriving iron industry until competition from larger Pennsylvania mines—with better access to post–Civil War markets—forced the local furnace to close. Now it's a bustling, upscale market town, its main street (US-7) lined with antique shops, galleries, and boutiques that have replaced blacksmith shops and wheelwrights. The area's transition from industry to leisure is implicit in the unusual displays inside the **Sloane-Stanley Museum** (Wed.–Sun. 10 AM–4 PM; $8; 860/927-3849), located along US-7 a mile north of Kent, near the ruins of an early-American iron foundry. The collection consists mainly of old tools—planes of all shapes and sizes, plus handsaws, augers, clamps, and other woodworking devices—all arranged by local artist and author Eric Sloane (1905–1985), whose books and prints are available in the gift shop. The "Stanley" in the museum's name comes (surprise, surprise) from the famous Stanley tool company, based in nearby New Britain, which donated the land and the museum building. Stanley tools make up a significant portion of the collection, but many others are handmade tools, some of which date back to days when colonial-era craftsmen forged their own tools to suit their specific needs.

Kent Falls State Park, along US-7 about four miles north of the museum, is a nice place to take a break from behind the wheel. Along with the namesake cascade, which is most impressive after a rain, the park includes a short path through dense woods.

Running south of Kent, parallel to US-7 for about six miles along the west bank of the Housatonic River, Schagticoke Road is a slower, much more scenic route that gives an up-close look at the rugged geology beneath the trees. The route crosses the Schagticoke Indian Reservation and passes an old Indian cemetery before rejoining US-7 via a covered bridge on Bulls Bridge Road, three miles north of Gaylordsville.

The Appalachian Trail crosses the New York state line near Bull's Bridge south of Kent, and so should you, making your way west to Route 22 or the Taconic State Parkway if you want to enjoy a landscape that offers more fields and trees than guardrails and parking lots. Technically speaking, there's still a large swath of New England between New York and New Milford, but most of this has more in common with the Indianapolis beltway than with the Vermont countryside.

NEW YORK

According to the map, the Appalachian Trail's corner-cutting path across the southern edge of the state seems well outside New York City's sprawl, but there is no escape from the greater

reality of the urban northeast: This part of the Atlantic seaboard is the original megalopolis. The map may not make it obvious that some tens of millions of people live within an hour's drive of this route, but the volume of traffic will.

Between the Connecticut border and the Hudson River, many of the roads along the route of the Appalachian Trail have become heavily developed corridors of suburban malls and Park and Ride lots for Manhattan commuters, but there are also some fascinating parks and other places worth exploring.

West Point

The hikers' Appalachian Trail, and our driving equivalent along old US-6, both cross the Hudson River near West Point, the U.S. Army's famous military academy, located at a point on the west bank of the Hudson, naturally. Even if you're not a military buff, there's a lot of fascinating history here: this is the fortress the traitorous U.S. General Benedict Arnold offered to hand over to the British (for cash and a promotion) during the Revolutionary War. There's a small museum (daily; free) offering guided tours of the grounds; walk up to Trophy Point for a great view of the river and a display of cannons captured during various U.S. wars.

On the north side of West Point, south of Newburgh off Hwy-32, stretch your legs and enjoy a different outlook on life at the pastoral **Storm King Art Center** (Apr.–mid-Nov. only, closed Mon. and Tues.; $10; 845/534-3115), a fabulous 500-acre sculpture park that celebrates the dynamic relationship between nature and culture. The artworks include more than a dozen large metal sculptures by the pioneering David Smith (1906–1965), who learned to weld while working in the Studebaker factory in South Bend, Indiana, and became one of the most influential Abstract Expressionists before his death in a car wreck. The Storm King collection also includes pieces by Alexander Calder, Henry Moore, and Louise Nevelson.

Even if you're racing across New York on the I-84 freeway, there's one place you should stop: the town of **Hyde Park**, where the homes of Franklin D. and Eleanor Roosevelt offer a look back at their admirable lives and challenging times.

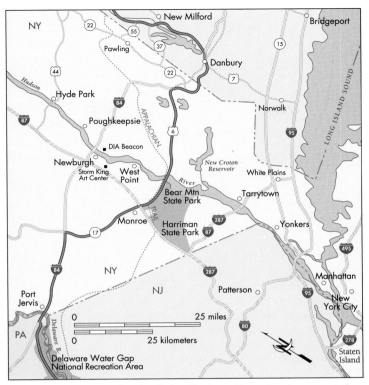

Along the east bank of the Hudson River in the town of Beacon, another unexpected art find is the intriguing **DIA Beacon** (closed Tues. & Wed.; $10; 845/440-0100), a minimally remodeled 1930s factory full of thought-provoking works by Robert Irwin, Dan Flavin, Donald Judd, Louise Bourgeois, Andy Warhol, and other artists. Metro-North commuter trains run right past the windows, heading down the river from Beacon to NYC's Grand Central Station (about 80 minutes each way; $25 round-trip).

West and south of West Point, the hikers' Appalachian Trail closely follows historic US-6 for a scenic foray through Harriman and Bear Mountain State Parks before heading south and west toward New Jersey and Pennsylvania.

Harriman State Park and Bear Mountain

Rising out of the Hudson Valley, **Harriman State Park** is a mountainous oasis with 30 lakes and some 200 miles of hiking

New York City

Some people avoid New York City like the plague, but more than eight million others can't bear to leave the glorious buzzing mosaic that makes New York unique in the world. Love it or hate it, New York is New York, and this great metropolis is undeniably the capital of the capitalist world, with some of the best museums, the best shops, the best sights, and the best restaurants in the world.

There's not much point in our recommending a select few of New York's huge spectrum of attractions, so we'll get straight to offering some practical help. For drivers, to whom all roads must seem to converge upon—and become gridlocked in—New York City, if you value your sanity and your shock absorbers: park your car in a long-term lot (not on the streets; city parking regulations are arcane and the fines huge) and walk or take public transportation. New York's subway system, one of the most extensive in the world, is relatively safe and usually the fastest way to get around town; it's also inexpensive ($2.25 per ride, or $8 a day, payable via electronic Metrocard). City buses are generally slower, but you see more of the sights. Taxis are ubiquitous—except when you want one.

The key to a successful visit to New York City is finding a place to stay. Ideally, you'll have an expense account, a friend, or a rich aunt, but lacking that, here are a few suggestions, most in the low-to-moderate range. It's hard to beat the **Holiday Inn Soho** ($225 and up; 212/966-8898) at 138 Lafayette Street for convenience, as it's equidistant from Chinatown, Little Italy, SoHo, and TriBeCa. For families, another good option is the **Embassy Suites,** 102 North End Avenue ($299 and up; 212/945-0100) at Battery Park City, with views of the Statue of Liberty. The least expensive

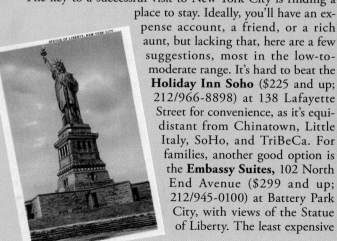

STATUE OF LIBERTY, NEW YORK CITY

place in town is the very large and popular **HI-New York Hostel** (212/932-2300), on the Upper West Side at 891 Amsterdam Avenue at 103rd Street, with private rooms (around $75) plus dorm beds for less than $40 a night. One of the many fabulous hotels in New York City is the small, stylish, and recently renovated Ian Shrager hotel, **Morgans** ($299 and up; 212/686-0300) at 237 Madison Avenue.

Eating out is another way to blow a lot of money very quickly, but there are some great places where you can get both a good meal and a feel for New York without going bankrupt. One such place is **Katz's Delicatessen,** 205 E. Houston Street (212/254-2246), a Lower East Side landmark that's been serving up man-sized sandwiches (including great pastrami) since 1888. (For movie buffs, Katz's is where Meg Ryan did her famous fake-orgasm scene in When Harry Met Sally.) And if you like diners, check out the **Empire Diner** (212/243-2736), at 210 10th Avenue at 22nd Street in the Chelsea neighborhood—all black enamel and gleaming stainless steel, and open 24 hours, 7 days a week. Another affordable all-American experience can be had at the retro-trendy **Shake Shack,** a high-style burger stand with two branches: outdoors in Madison Square Park, a leafy oasis off Madison Avenue at E. 23rd Street (212/889-6600), and on the Upper West Side near the Museum of Natural History at 366 Columbus Avenue (646/747-8770). On the Upper East Side, between the Metropolitan and Whitney museums, Michelin-starred chef Daniel Boulud serves up exquisitely prepared French bistro fare at his **Cafe Boulud,** 20 E. 76th Street (212/772-2600). The ever-changing menu features a wide variety of traditional favorites and contemporary inventions, available for lunch and dinner at (comparatively) moderate prices. It's very popular, so make reservations as soon as you can.

trails; the first section of the Appalachian Trail was opened here in 1923. In utter contrast to the get-out-of-my-way style of later highway construction, the roads across the park, designed in the 1920s for Sunday afternoon family outings in the newfangled motor car, maximize exposure to the surrounding forests, and even the rustic Romanesque stone arch bridges manage to harmonize with local rock outcroppings.

Bear Mountain Bridge carries the Appalachian Trail across the Hudson River.

Closer to the Hudson River, an adjacent state park, **Bear Mountain,** is even more full of old-fashioned pleasures and draws more annual visitors than Yellowstone National Park (no doubt thanks to its location at the north end of the Palisades Parkway). A scenic drive leads near the top of Bear Mountain itself, where a New Deal–era lookout tower gives views over the entire region, and an interior mural traces local history. In season, there are pedal boats for rent, plus a large swimming pool (or an ice-skating rink). Meals and accommodations are available in the circa-1915 **Bear Mountain Inn** (845/786-2731).

About 30 miles northwest of Port Jervis, Max Yasgur's farm outside **Bethel, New York,** welcomed revelers to the August 1969 Woodstock Festival of Music and Art, starring Jimi Hendrix; Crosby, Stills and Nash; and some 300,000 mud-soaked hippies.

Local literary trivia: At the beginning of Jack Kerouac's *On the Road,* the main character, Sal Paradise, sets off from New York City on an ill-fated attempt to follow US-6 all the way to the West Coast. Hoping to hitch a ride along the "one red line called Route 6 that led from the tip of Cape Cod clear to Ely, Nevada, and there dipped down to Los Angeles," Sal got caught in a rainstorm here at Bear Mountain and had to head home, giving up on the "stupid hearthside idea that it would be wonderful to fol-

low one great line across America instead of trying various roads and routes."

Port Jervis

West of Harriman State Park, the Appalachian Trail and US-6 cross the busy I-87 New York Thruway, then wind through the exurbs of the Big Apple, where town after town seems unsure whether this is country living or not.

Farther west, along I-84 on the tri-state (NY/NJ/PA) border, **Port Jervis** is a curious mixture of small-town dereliction and commercial bustle. Transportation has clearly been a major historical force here, with the influence of successive eras—the river, the railroad, and the highway—inscribed in the very layout of the town. For a glimpse of the long reign of the iron horse, check out the intriguing artifacts and photos in the restored waiting room of the old **Erie Lackawanna Depot** on Front Street, or stop inside the old **Erie Hotel** next door, which has an ornate bar, a lively restaurant and rooms upstairs ($60; 845/858-4100).

Port Jervis clearly still believes in the virtues of home cooking: **Homer's Coffee Shop** (845/856-1712), unmissable at 2 E. Main Street, is a prime example, with its democratic social club of elderly regulars, young tie-wearing businessmen, and tradespeople with company names stitched on their shirt pockets, all drawn to the bargain meals and early-morning doughnuts. Despite the acoustic tile and too-new counter and seating, it's a welcoming spot, with the added attraction of a soda fountain in case you need to wash down that turkey club or beef stroganoff with a Tin Roof Sundae.

PENNSYLVANIA

The hikers' Appalachian Trail runs across southern New York and western New Jersey, but our road route avoids the Garden State almost entirely, crossing instead the natural chasm of the **Delaware Water Gap,** whose forests, waterfalls, and wildlife are popular with city-dwellers escaping the New York–Philly megalopolis. In its 150-mile length, this route across Pennsylvania passes through a succession of strikingly different

places, starting with the densely populated industrial regions of the Lehigh Valley and the historic little town of **Bethlehem,** which plays up its Christmas connections more than its role as a formerly vital steelmaking center. Farther south, modern industry gives way to the traditional agriculture of **Pennsylvania Dutch Country,** world famous for its anti-technology, Old Order Christian communities. Continuing southwest across the Susquehanna River, you'll follow the route of the old Lincoln Highway through historic **York,** early capital of the United States, now home to the Harley-Davidson motorcycle assembly plant. The last stop on the Pennsylvania leg of the route is the Civil War battlefields at **Gettysburg,** just shy of the Maryland border.

Lackawaxen

The tiny town of **Lackawaxen** (pop. 125), along the Delaware River 20 winding, scenic miles northwest of Port Jervis via Hwy-97, holds two fascinating attractions: the preserved home of writer Zane Grey, and a unique suspension bridge built in 1847 by Brooklyn Bridge designer John Roebling. It comes as

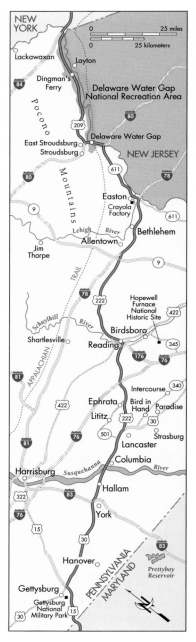

something of a surprise to find out that Zane Grey, author of the classic Western novel *Riders of the Purple Sage,* was in fact a fly-fishing, baseball-loving Pennsylvania dentist, but he was. His home at 135 Scenic Drive was preserved by his family as the **Zane Grey Museum** (Fri.–Sun. 10 AM–5 PM; free; 570/685-4871) and now offers an intimate look into his life and works. Zane Grey and his wife (and childhood sweetheart) Dolly are buried side-by-side in the small Lackawaxen graveyard.

The Roebling Bridge is about 100 yards downstream from Zane Grey's home and has been preserved by the National Park Service—though it's now used by cars instead of canal boats. For the full experience, stay the night in the circa-1860 canal office, now housing the **Roebling Inn** ($99 and up; 570/685-7900).

Milford

At the west end of US-6's very pleasant run along the river from Port Jervis, just off I-84 at the northern end of Delaware Water Gap National Recreation Area, **Milford** (pop. 1,400) is a cute little town cashing in on the hordes of rafters, campers, and B&B patrons who make the weekend journey to the surrounding Pocono Mountains from New York or Philadelphia.

Milford was the longtime home of sustainable forestry pioneer and two-term Pennsylvania Governor Gifford Pinchot (1865-1946), whose **Grey Towers** estate off US-6 is now preserved as a National Historic Site, open in summer for tours ($5; 570/296-9630). Visitors and locals alike converge on the town's culinary landmark, the **Milford Diner** at 301 Broad Street (6 AM–10 PM daily; 570/296-8611).

Delaware Water Gap National Recreation Area

Totaling some 70,000 acres of forest on both banks of the Delaware River, the **Delaware Water Gap National Recreation Area** stretches for 35 miles south of the I-84 freeway along two-lane US-209. Established in 1965, the park is still very much under development, though numerous hiking trails lead through hardwood forests to seasonal waterfalls, and the river itself offers abundant canoeing, swimming, and fishing. Though far from pristine, the natural beauty is surprisingly undisturbed considering the park lies only 50 miles west of New York City.

A few remnants of the area's historic agricultural villages have

been preserved under the aegis of the park service, but the main attraction is the oddly named Delaware Water Gap itself, a deep cleft carved by the river into the solid rock of the Kittatinny Mountains. Artists, sightseers, and rock-climbers have admired this unique feat of geology for centuries, but unfortunately the natural passageway is crisscrossed by all manner of road and railroad, including the six-lane I-80 freeway that runs right through it.

The tiny tourist town of **Delaware Water Gap,** south of I-80 at the far southern end of the park, provides the best views of the gap. A visitors center sits along the river, just off I-80 at the first/last New Jersey exit, and offers exhibits on the geology and history of the region. Also in town is **Pack Shack Adventures,** a block off the Appalachian Trail at 88 Broad Street (570/424-8533), where you can rent a canoe, get out on the water, and stretch your arms and legs.

The Poconos

The **Pocono Mountains,** which rise to the west of the Delaware River, hold a number of traditional summer resort hotels spread among the golf courses and ski areas. Like the Catskills "Borscht Belt" of southern New York, the Poconos had their glory days in the 1950s, but some resorts still thrive thanks to the invention here in the 1960s of the couple-friendly, heart- or champagne glass–shaped bath tub, which has turned many a Pocono hotel into a pseudo-Roman honeymoon destination (the *Baltimore Sun* called one a "mini Playboy Mansion"). Many of these pas-

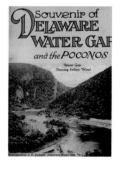

A 25-mile stretch of the Appalachian Trail cuts along a 1,200-foot-high ridge at the southeast corner of the park, crossing the Delaware River on an old bridge at the town of Delaware Water Gap. Get a feel for the trail at the full-service, AMC-run **Mohican Outdoor Center** (908/362-5670), outside Blairstown, New Jersey.

sion pits tend to feature all-inclusive package deals (free archery lessons, so you and your beloved can play Cupid with real arrows, etc). If you're interested, try **Caesars Pocono Palace** (800/432-9932) off US-209 five miles northeast of Stroudsburg.

By contrast, a classic "old-school" Pocono resort—the rightly named **Skytop** (800/345-7759)—is about 20 miles northwest of Stroudsburg, via Hwy-447. This very grand yet family-friendly 1920s hotel, with just 150 rooms but full resort facilities, sits on 6,000 acres of mountaintop forest, with its own golf course, hiking trails, and hunting preserve.

At the southern edge of the Delaware Water Gap park, **Stroudsburg** has the Poconos' most extensive tourist facilities, clustered along the I-80 freeway corridor.

Easton and Nazareth

South of the Delaware Water Gap, Hwy-611 runs along the Delaware River until its confluence with the Lehigh River, near the town of **Easton.** This historic industrial center is now home to one of the Poconos' most popular family attractions: the **Crayola Crayon Factory Tour** (closed Mon.; $9; 610/515-8000), at 30 Center Square, where you can watch colorful crayons being made and packaged, then scribble away to your heart's content. The actual Crayola factory is a half dozen miles away and not open to the public; this toddler-friendly mini-factory shares a waterfront building with the **National Canal Museum,** which traces the history of the Delaware and Lehigh Canal and other man-made waterways all over the United States. Occasional canal boat trips are offered.

Along with Martin Guitars, Nazareth is home to **Nazareth Speedway,** home track of the Andretti racing family. Another sporting hero, boxer Larry Holmes, lives in Easton.

Another more historic American factory tour is in nearby **Nazareth,** where the venerable **Martin Guitar Company** (610/867-0173 or 800/633-2060) has been in business since 1833. If you've

ever enjoyed strumming a six-string, you'll want to take one of the wonderful tours (Mon.–Fri. at 1:15 PM; free) of the family-owned factory at 510 Sycamore Street. The tours include both a look inside the workshops—where you can watch workers as they bend, carve, inlay, and polish the instruments—and displays of classic Martin guitars.

Bethlehem

Upstream from Easton along the Lehigh River and US-222, the remarkable small city of **Bethlehem** (pop. 71,329), famous for its Christmas festivals and as a fun place from which to mail Christmas cards, was originally established in 1741 by a group of Moravian missionaries. The missionaries' original circa-1803 chapel still stands at the heart of the compact, gaslighted downtown district, its cemetery full of 200-year-old headstones laid flat so as not to offend God.

The **Moravian Museum,** at 66 W. Church Street (610/867-0173), is housed inside the circa-1741 *Gemeinhaus,* the oldest building in Bethlehem. Besides showcasing historic artifacts, the museum also offers guided walking tours of the downtown area. Another engaging historic site is the **Sun Inn** at 564 Main Street, a well-preserved former tavern "where the leading figures of the Revolutionary era were entertained," says a plaque on the wall.

Across the Lehigh River from the tidy homes and shops of downtown Bethlehem, Lehigh University stands above the rusting remains of the Bethlehem Steel Company. Famous for fabricating engineering marvels such as the towers of the Golden Gate Bridge—cast here in sections, then shipped through the Panama Canal and assembled in San Francisco—the mill was in business for over a century before being closed down in 1995. The hulking structure, the massive blast furnace, and most of the cranes and other machinery and equipment are slated for preservation as part of the Smithsonian Institution's National Museum of Industrial History,

Every May, Bethlehem hosts a hugely popular **Bach Festival,** rated as one of the best in country. For details, contact the Bach Choir at 610/866-4382.

while the bulk of the complex is being converted into the massive "Sands BethWorks"casino, which opened in 2009.

Along with the old steel works and the new casino, the Lehigh University neighborhood holds another noteworthy landmark: the non-profit **Godfrey Daniels Coffee House,** 7 E. 4th Street (610/867-2390), which has been hosting a range of live folk and jazz music for more than 30 years. For a bite to eat, grab a chili dog at **Pete's,** around the corner at 400 Broadway (610/866-6622), or head back across the river into Bethlehem proper, where the bistro-style **Apollo,** 85 W. Broad Street (610/865-9600) is perhaps the nicest place in town for lunch or dinner.

For a place to stay, the large **Hotel Bethlehem** ($110–135; 610/625-5000 or 800/333-3333), at 437 Main Street overlooking the river, is centrally located.

Allentown

The seat of Lehigh County, **Allentown** (pop. 106,632) spreads west of Bethlehem, across a bend in the Lehigh River. The downtown area has two very worthwhile stops, the bigger and better of which is the **Allentown Art Museum** (closed Mon.; $6; 610/432-4333) at 31 N. 5th Street. Here you'll find a good general collection of paintings and photography as well as an entire library moved from the Frank Lloyd Wright–designed Little House. Allentown's other main attraction lies two blocks west at Church and Hamilton Streets: the **Liberty Bell Shrine** (Mon.–Sat. noon–4 PM; free), an old church that houses a replica of the famous bell that was hidden here for safekeeping during the Revolutionary War battles at Philadelphia.

Allentown boasts some great places to eat, thanks to the multiple branches of **Yocco's: The Hot Dog King;** these local landmarks, like the one at 625 Liberty Street (610/433-1950), have been serving up wieners (and a few burgers) bathed in

The town of **Jim Thorpe,** in the Lehigh Valley 30 miles northwest of Allentown off the Pennsylvania Turnpike (Hwy-9), 10 miles north of the Appalachian Trail, is a former coal-mining town with many 19th-century buildings. The town changed its name from Mauch Chunk in 1954 to honor the great Olympic athlete Jim Thorpe, whose remains lie in a granite mausoleum along Hwy-903 on the northeast side of town.

Another reason to visit: the Class AAA **Lehigh Valley Ironpigs,** the Phillies top farm club, play in a nice new ballpark ($7–14; 610/841-PIGS), south of US-22 near the Allentown airport. Games are broadcast on **1470 AM.**

Midway between Allentown and Reading, every June and July the weeklong **Kutztown Folk Festival** celebrates the arts, crafts, and culture of the local Pennsylvania Dutch communities, which are less austere than their Lancaster County counterparts.

A step below their near neighbors the Ironpigs, Reading is home to another Phillies farm club, the **R-Phils,** who play AA-ball at the very pleasant FirstEnergy Field ($7–10; 610/375-8469). Games are on **1240 AM.**

a top-secret chili sauce since 1922. Allentown also has one of the country's oldest, largest collections of roller coasters (and a fine old carousel), in **Dorney Park** (daily in summer; around $40; 610/395-3724). There's a water park, too.

Reading

Standing along the eastern banks of the Schuylkill River, **Reading** (pop. 83,463) is more interesting than its frightening title, "Factory Outlet Shopping Capital of Southeastern Pennsylvania," might lead you to expect. Ornately turreted row houses line 5th Avenue (US-222 Business) through the residential districts, downtown holds a number of well-maintained businesses and signs from the first half of the 20th century, and a very photogenic 85-foot, 100-year-old pagoda offers panoramic views from the summit of Mt. Penn, east of town.

For history buffs, two worthwhile places to visit sit southeast of Reading along the Schuylkill River. The closer of these is at **Birdsboro,** 10 miles from town and a mile north of US-422. The **Daniel Boone Homestead and Birthplace** (closed Mon.; $4; 610/582-4900) marks the site where the great frontiersman was born in 1734.

Well worth the winding five-mile drive south of Birdsboro via Hwy-345, the **Hopewell Furnace National Historic Site** (daily; $4) preserves intact an entire iron-making community

The Monopoly "Chance" card "Take a Ride on the Reading," commemorates the railroad that formerly ran between Reading and Philadelphia.

that thrived here from the colonial era until the mid-1880s. Park rangers fire up the furnace and demonstrate the primitive foundry (melting aluminum rather than iron to take the "heat" off the ancient tools), and exhibits trace the iron-making process—mining the ore, making charcoal, and fabricating the finished product, which here at Hopewell was primarily pig iron and stoves.

Roadside America

One of the quirkiest tourist attractions in the United States, Roadside America (daily; $6; 610/488-6241) stands alongside the I-78 freeway, 20 miles northwest of Reading in the village of Shartlesville. Built by Reading native Laurence Gieringer, Roadside America is a giant ⅜-to-the-inch scale model of bygone Americana, fleshed out with animated scenes that trace a typical day in the life of the country—circa 1941, when Roadside America first opened to the public. As you walk around the edges of the 8,000-square-foot exhibit, you can push buttons to make wheels spin, lights flash, and pumps pump, and you'll see a little of everything rural: an 1830s New England village featuring a church and choral music; a canyon and lake complete with waterfalls and resort cabins; a model of Henry Ford's workshop in Dearborn, Michigan, where he built one of the first "horseless carriages"; various turnpikes, canals, highways, and railroads; a coal mine; and a mock-up of the San Francisco Bay Bridge, the closest Roadside comes to a city scene.

Though it's definitely a fine example of kitsch, Roadside America is also an oddly compelling place, and only the hardest-hearted road-tripper will be able to hold back the tears when, every half hour or so, the sun sets and Kate Smith bursts into "God Bless America."

Ephrata and Lititz

South of Reading, US-222 runs along the western edge of the Amish- and Mennonite-influenced Pennsylvania Dutch Country. The heart of this region is due east of Lancaster, but the area north of Lancaster also holds a number of related sites often missed by

Ephrata Cloister

The Pennsylvania Dutch Country

East of Lancaster, toward Philadelphia, the old Lincoln Highway (US-30) runs through the heart of what has become internationally famous as the Pennsylvania Dutch Country. This is a very pretty, almost completely rural region, unremarkable apart from the presence here of various "Old Order" Anabaptist Christian sects, including Amish and Mennonite groups, who eschew most of the trappings and technological advances of the 21st century, including cars, electricity, and irrigation, and retain their simple ways. Long before the Peter Weir movie *Witness* gave Amish low-tech lifestyle the Hollywood treatment, visitors have been coming here to see these anachronistic descendants of German immigrants (Deutsche = Dutch) who settled here in the early 1700s, and to whom all outsiders are known simply as "English."

The best way to get a feel for the Amish and Mennonite ways of life is to follow back roads, by bike if possible, through the gently rolling countryside of Lancaster County, keeping an eye out for their horse-drawn buggies (Amish ones are gray, the Mennonites' are black). You can cross covered bridges, or buy produce, breads, cakes, and "Shoo

Amish Boys Out for a Drive, Lancaster County, Pa.

visitors. The most appealing of these is the **Ephrata Cloister** (daily; $9), at 632 W. Main Street just west of the town of Ephrata. Founded in 1732 by a communal society of religiously celibate German Pietists, the Ephrata Cloister consists of a half dozen well-preserved 250-year-old wooden buildings, which housed dormitories, bakeries, and a printing shop where the commune produced some of the finest illustrated books of the colonial era. Across Main Street from the entrance, the **Cloister Restaurant** (717/733-2361) serves very good home-

A word to the wise: In Dutch Country, remember that anything claiming to be **"authentic Amish"** definitely isn't. Please respect the Amish you see and refrain from taking photographs. Drive carefully, too.

Fly Pie" from the many roadside stands marked by hand-lettered signs. If you're fond of kitsch, don't miss the restored one-room **Weavertown Schoolhouse** ($4), populated by "authentic" audio-animatronic Amish schoolkids, along Hwy-340 a mile east of the town of Bird-in-Hand, 2.5 miles west of Intercourse.

Most of the many Amish-style restaurants in the region are huge and forbiddingly full of bus-tour hordes; one exception is **Stoltzfus Restaurant** (May–Nov. Mon.–Sat. 11 AM–8 PM; 717/768-8156) on Hwy-772 a mile southeast of Intercourse. A less Amish but very good road-food place is **Jennie's Diner** in Ronks, open 24 hours every day on the north side of US-30 at 2575 E. Lincoln Highway (717/397-2507), just east of the Hwy-896 intersection.

Though it won't give you any great insight into the Amish, one unique place to stay is the **Red Caboose Motel and Restaurant** ($85 and up; 717/687-5000), a mile east of Strasburg on Paradise Lane. All the rooms are built inside old railroad cars, and the on-site restaurant simulates a train journey, with whistles blowing and a gentle rocking vibration to ease your digestion. Strasburg is also home to the **Village Greens** miniature golf course (717/687-6933), which is so fun and challenging that it was featured in *Sports Illustrated*.

For complete listings of attractions, restaurants, and hotels, or to pick up handy maps and other information, stop by the helpful **Pennsylvania Dutch Visitor Center** (800/PA-DUTCH), on US-30 just east of Lancaster.

style food for breakfast, lunch, and dinner in an overgrown 1940s diner.

If you happen, or can manage, to be in Ephrata on a Friday, there's no more authentic Dutch Country experience than the once-a-week **Green Dragon Farmers Market** (717/738-1117), a chaotic complex of some 400 different fresh fruit and vegetable sellers, sausage and hot dog stands, pizza places, and bakery outlets, covering 30 acres in seven buildings, just over a mile north of town at 955 N. State

Lititz is the unlikely final resting place of **John Sutter,** the Swiss immigrant who owned huge chunks of pre–gold rush California. He died here in Pennsylvania while battling the Washington, D.C. bureaucracy, hoping to receive compensation for his confiscated land.

Street. Many people here are truly Amish, so obey the 2nd commandment and resist the urge to take their photo.

West of Ephrata, eight miles north of Lancaster via Hwy-501, the delightful though tiny town of **Lititz** (pop. 8,280) is dominated by the huge **Wilbur Chocolate** candy factory at 48 N. Broad Street, which liberally perfumes the air with the smell of hot chocolate. Lititz, which is packed full of stone buildings and carefully tended gardens, also holds the nation's oldest operating pretzel factory, the **Sturgis Pretzel House** at 219 E. Main Street, where you can twist your own. Lititz also holds a huge 4th of July party every year—well worth planning a trip around.

Lancaster

The only place approaching an urban scale in this part of Pennsylvania, **Lancaster** (pop. 56,438) is the region's commercial center, a bustling city that, for a single day during the Revolutionary War, served as capital of the country. Though most visitors view it as little more than a handy base for exploring nearby Pennsylvania Dutch Country, Lancaster does have a couple of attractions in its own right, such as the redbrick, pseudo-Romanesque **Central Market** at King and Queen Streets in the center of town. It hosts the nation's oldest publicly owned, continuously operating farmers market, currently held all day Tuesday and Friday, as well as Saturday mornings. A block south on Queen Street, the ground-floor windows of the local newspaper trace local history through headlines, starting back in 1794 and continuing up through the present day.

Two miles northeast of Lancaster, the state-run and well-signed **Landis Valley Museum** (daily; $12) is a popular 40-acre living history park preserving and interpreting traditional rural life ways of eastern Pennsylvania.

Hallam: The Shoe House

Many oddball attractions grew up along the old Lincoln Highway, the great cross-country highway that ran coast-to-coast beginning in 1915, and one of the best-beloved is the **Haines Shoe House,** which stands above the modern four-lane US-30 freeway, west of the town of Hallam. This landmark of programmatic architecture was built in 1948 by Mahlon "The Shoe Wizard" Haines, who owned a successful shoe company that proudly claimed to make boots "hoof-to-hoof," from raising the cattle to selling the finished products.

The seven-room structure is shaped like a giant cartoon boot and can be reached by following Hwy-462 (the old Lincoln Highway, which runs just south of current US-30), to Shoe House Road, then winding north for a quarter mile. (The turnoff is easy to miss, so keep an eye out for the Shoe House Mini-Storage, which stands on the corner.) The Shoe House has been bought and sold a number of times over the years. If you're lucky, the owners will be there to let you tour the interior.

Just east of Hallam on US-30, **Jim Mack's Ice Cream** (717/252-2013) at 5745 Lincoln Highway has been attracting fans for its ice cream—and its adjacent mini-golf course and mini-zoo, complete with a pair of rather sad-looking brown bears. Next door: a bowling alley.

Two of the main tourist stops in the Dutch Country region are the towns of **Intercourse** (source of many snickeringly allusive postcards) and **Paradise** (the Paradise post office, just north of US-30 at the east end of town, is a popular place for sending mail).

Midway between Lancaster and York, the town of **Columbia** holds what is arguably the country's best collection of timepieces in the **Watch and Clock Museum** at 514 Poplar Street. Also in Columbia is a beautiful multi-arched concrete bridge that used to carry the old Lincoln Highway (US-30) across the broad Susquehanna River.

York

Though it doesn't look like much from the highway, bypassed by both US-30 and the I-83 freeway, the medium-sized town of **York** (pop. 40,862) claims to be the first capital of the United States: Late in 1777, the Articles of Confederation were adopted here by the 13 newly independent former colonies, and (arguably) it's in that document that the name "United States of America" was first used. A significant number of historic buildings still stand in the quiet, low-rise downtown area, including the medieval-looking, circa-1740 Golden Plough Tavern and other colonial-era structures along Market Street at the west edge of the business district.

For all its historic importance, York is best known for its industrial prowess, which is saluted at the **Harley-Davidson assembly plant and museum** (Mon.–Fri. 9 AM–2 PM; free;

717/852-6590), a mile east of town off US-30 on Eden Road. The guided tours take about two hours and begin with a brief history of the company, which is still based in Milwaukee. The tour then takes you past a lineup of some 40 Harleys past and present, culled from the corporate collection of over 200 motorbikes, then proceeds to the shop floor for a close-up (and very noisy) look and listen as the bikes get put together: Sheets of steel are pressed to form fenders and fairings, and, once assembled, each bike is "road-tested" at full throttle on motorcycling's equivalent of a treadmill. A souvenir store is stocked with all manner of things with the Harley-Davidson logo, from T-shirts to leather jackets.

Downtown York has a handful of cafés and restaurants, and on the west edge of town, where the US-30 bypass rejoins the old Lincoln Highway (Hwy-462), **Lee's Diner** (717/792-1300), at 4320 W. Market Street, is a classic early 1950s Mountain View pre-fab diner, still serving up hearty road food. The nicest place to stay has to be the historic **Yorktowne Hotel,** 48 E. Market Street ($119 and up; 717/848-1111), a 1920s landmark.

Gettysburg

Totally overwhelmed by the influx of tourists visiting its namesake battleground, the town of **Gettysburg** (pop. 7,490) has survived both onslaughts remarkably unscathed. Despite the presence of sundry tourist attractions—wax museums, various multimedia reenactments of the battle and President Lincoln's Gettysburg Address, even a Lincoln Train Museum displaying over a thousand model trains that include a scale replica of the one Lincoln rode

Abraham Lincoln
Robert E. Lee
George Gordon Meade

here in—once the day-tripping crowds have dispersed, Gettysburg is actually a very pleasant place, with rows of brick-fronted buildings lining Baltimore and York streets at the center of town.

There are, not surprisingly, quite a few places to eat, including the atmospheric **Dobbin House,** (717/334-2100) south of town at 89 Steinwehr Avenue, serving above-average pub food in Gettysburg's oldest building. The same building doubles as the **Gettystown Inn** ($95 and up; 717/334-2100), a moderately priced and pleasant B&B. The dozens of other places to stay include all the usual national chains, plus the circa-1797 **Gettysburg Hotel** ($95 and up; 717/337-2000) on Lincoln Square right at the center of town.

Gettysburg National Military Park

Site of the most famous two-minute speech in U.S. history, and of the bloody Civil War battle that marked the high tide of Confederate fortunes, **Gettysburg National Military Park** surrounds the town of Gettysburg, protecting the scenes of the struggle as they were July 1–3, 1863, when 50,000 of the 165,000 combatants were killed or wounded. Over a thousand monuments mark the various historic sites around the 6,000 acres of rolling green pasture that form the park. The entire battlefield is evocative and interesting, but to make the most of a visit start your tours at the **visitors center** (daily; free; 717/334-1124), discreetly hidden away on Hunt Avenue east of Taneytown Road two miles south of town, where an extensive museum puts the battle into context and displays a huge array of period weaponry. Unfortunately, you can no longer watch the battle unfold on the much-loved Electric Map, which looks a lot like a boxing ring but has been superceded by more advanced multimedia displays in the digital age. However, the new visitors center has made space for an even older didactic artifact: the famous circular **Cyclorama,** a 26-by 356-foot painting that evocatively portrays the events of the final day's battles. There are also numerous maps and guides available, including an excellent podcast tour of the surrounding battleground.

The town of **Hanover,** south of US-30 between York and Gettysburg, is a prime producer of snack foods, from potato chips to the famed pretzels baked by **Snyder's of Hanover,** 1350 York Street, which offers free factory tours.

A 230-acre farm on the southwest fringe of the Gettysburg battlefields was home to U.S. Army general and later-president **Dwight D. Eisenhower** and his wife, Mamie, and is now open for guided tours (daily; $7; 717/338-9114) that leave from the Gettysburg visitors center.

The Lincoln Highway

The main east–west route through Pennsylvania Dutch Country, US-30 is also one of the best-preserved stretches of the old Lincoln Highway, the nation's first transcontinental route. Planned and named in 1915, linking New York City's Times Square with the Panama Pacific International Exposition in San Francisco, the Lincoln Highway followed over 3,000 miles of country road across 12 states. A thousand miles of the original "highway" were little more than muddy tracks, scarcely more visible on the ground than they were on the still-nonexistent road maps, but by the early 1930s the road was finally fully paved, following present-day US-30 as far as Wyoming, then bending south to follow what's now US-50, "The Loneliest Road in America," along the route of the Pony Express across Nevada and most of California.

Originally marked by telephone poles brightly painted with red, white, and blue stripes and a large letter "L," in 1928 the Lincoln Highway was blazed by more discreet concrete mileposts carrying a small bust of Lincoln; 3,000 of these were placed, one every mile, by Boy Scout troops across the land, but only around a dozen still stand in the original locations. As with the later Route 66, the Lincoln Highway was replaced by the Interstates, but it does live on, in folk memory as well as the innumerable Lincoln Cafes and Lincoln Motels along its original route, much of which still bears the name Lincolnway. You can become a member of the **Lincoln Highway Association** (815/456-3030), which offers a top-quality quarterly magazine well worth the annual dues.

North from the visitors center, a mile-long and very worth-while walk leads north to the **Gettysburg National Cemetery,** where President Abraham Lincoln delivered his famous address on November 19, 1863.

MARYLAND

Crossing the Mason-Dixon Line from Gettysburg into Maryland on US-15, our route veers west into the Appalachian foothills of **Catoctin Mountain Park,** site of the presidential retreat Camp David. The landscape here is quite rugged, and signs of life few and far between—an oasis of peace and quiet, under an hour by road from Baltimore or Washington, D.C. Winding south through the mountains of the Maryland Panhandle (the thin strip of land that stretches for some 75 miles between Pennsylvania and West Virginia), this route again meets the hikers' Appalachian Trail, then detours to visit the battlefield of **Antietam,** the well-preserved site of the worst carnage of the Civil War.

The Maryland state motto, *Fatti Maschii, Parole Femine,* is translated roughly as "Manly Deeds, Womanly Words."

Catoctin Mountain Park: Camp David

US-15 continues south from Gettysburg across the Maryland border, and there's little to stop for until **Thurmont** (pop. 5,588), "Gateway to the Mountains." The green expanse of **Catoctin Mountain Park,** fully recovered after previous centuries of logging activity, protects some 10,000 acres of hardwood forest, a handful of 1,500-foot peaks, and the presidential retreat at Camp David, hidden away in the woods and strictly off-limits to visitors (for security reasons, Camp David doesn't even appear on park maps). The **Catoctin park visitors center** (daily; 301/663-9388) along Hwy-77 two miles west of US-15 provides information on cabins, camping, and maps of the many hiking trails, including a short trail from the visitors center to the preserved remains of the

In Gathland State Park, on the Appalachian Trail east of Gapland off Hwy-67, the 50-foot terra-cotta arch of the **War Correspondents Memorial** was erected in the late 1880s in honor of journalists killed while covering the Civil War.

The name "David" in Camp David was bestowed by President Eisenhower in celebration of his then 5-year-old grandson, who went on to marry Julie Nixon, daughter of Eisenhower's VP, Richard Nixon. Later in life, young David also inspired John Fogerty of Creedence Clearwater Revival to write the song "Fortunate Son."

Blue Blazes whiskey still, where rangers demonstrate moonshine-making on summer weekends.

Spreading along the south side of Hwy-77, Maryland-run **Cunningham Falls State Park** offers more natural scenery and a very pleasant swimming area in Hunting Creek Lake. There's a snack bar and boats for rent, and a half-mile trail leads to the eponymous cascade.

Washington Monument State Park

From Catoctin Mountain Park, our route heads south on undivided Hwy-6 and two-lane Hwy-17 along the hikers' Appalachian Trail, winding up at **Washington Monument State Park** between the I-70 freeway and the small town of **Boonsboro.** A 35-foot-tall, bottle-shaped mound dedicated to the memory of George Washington stands at the center of the park; Boonsboro

citizens completed the monument in 1827, making it the oldest memorial honoring the first U.S. president.

Atop a hill south of the park, across an old alignment of the National Road (US-40), the **Old South Mountain Inn** (301/432-6155) has operated as a tavern and inn since 1732 and now serves dinner Tues.–Sun. and lunch on weekends.

Antietam National Battlefield

Between Boonsboro and the Potomac River, which forms Maryland's border with West Virginia, **Antietam National Battlefield** preserves the hallowed ground where over 23,000 men were killed or wounded on the bloodiest single day of the Civil War—September 17, 1862. Atop a shallow hill at the middle of the park, a scant mile north of **Sharpsburg** off Hwy-65, the **visitors center** (daily; $5 per car; 301/432-5124) offers films, museum exhibits, and interpretive programs that put the battle into military and political context. Though there was no clear winner, Antietam is said to have convinced Lincoln to issue the Emancipation Proclamation, officially freeing slaves in Confederate states and effectively putting an end to British support for the southern side.

Clara Barton tended the wounded during and after the Civil War's bloodiest battle at Antietam.

WEST VIRGINIA

In its short run across the eastern tip of West Virginia, US-340 passes through one of the most history-rich small towns in the United States: **Harpers Ferry,** located at the confluence of the Shenandoah and Potomac Rivers. Lovely mountain scenery surrounds Harpers Ferry, especially during early autumn when the hardwood forests rival Vermont's for vibrant color. South of Harpers Ferry, the hikers' Appalachian Trail runs directly along the Virginia/West Virginia border, east of the Shenandoah River atop the roadless crest of the Blue Ridge Mountains. The best route to follow by car, US-340 swings to the west through the historic mountain resort of **Charles Town** before entering Virginia.

Harpers Ferry

Climbing the steep slopes of the Blue Ridge Mountains, **Harpers Ferry** (pop. 300) embodies the industrial and political history of the early United States. Protected since 1963 as a national park, its many well-preserved wood, brick, and stone buildings are palpable reminders of early American enterprise: Besides the country's first large factory, first canal, and first railroad, scenic Harpers Ferry saw abolitionist John Brown's

1859 rebellion against slavery, and it was later a strategic site during the Civil War. Harpers Ferry was also home to Storer College, an African American college that operated here from the 1860s until 1955.

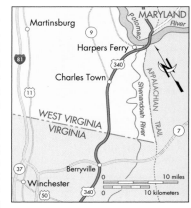

Small museums, housed in separate buildings along Shenandoah and High Streets along the riverfront in the "Lower Town," trace the various strands of the town's past. From the Shenandoah River, the Appalachian Trail winds south down what the third president called "one of the most stupendous scenes in Nature," Jefferson's Rock. Crossing the Potomac River to the north, the AT climbs up to Maryland Heights for more spectacular vistas.

Especially in summer, when cars are banned from lower Harpers Ferry, the best first stop is the small **visitors center** (daily; $5; 304/535-6223) above the town along US-340. Park here and take one of the frequent free shuttles down to the historic area. Although most of Harpers Ferry is preserved as a historic site, there is considerable pressure to "develop" surrounding lands, so get here while it's still nice. The eastern portions along the Potomac riverfront have remained in private hands, and here you can indulge your taste for fast food, wax museums, and schlocky souvenirs. There's excellent cycling, a couple of companies offer whitewater rafting trips, and for another sort of adventure you can hop onboard one of the **Amtrak/MARC** trains, which serve Washington, D.C., on a very limited schedule. To get the most out of a visit, stay overnight at the lovingly restored, circa-1790s, Federal-style, brick-fronted **Jackson Rose Inn,** 1167 W. Washington Street ($125 and up; 304/535-1528).

Harpers Ferry is the national headquarters of the **Appalachian Trail Conference,** the nonprofit group that oversees the entire 2,144-mile footpath. For information, contact the group at 304/535-6331.

Charles Town

Founded in 1786, the former colonial resort of **Charles Town** (pop. 2,907) was named in honor of George

Washington's younger brother Charles, who surveyed the site on behalf of Lord Fairfax. Many of the streets are named after other family members, over 75 of whom are buried in the cemetery alongside the **Zion Church,** on Congress Street on the east side of town. Charles Town, which shouldn't be confused with the West Virginia state capital, Charleston, later played a significant role in John Brown's failed raid on Harpers Ferry. After Brown was captured, he was tried and convicted of treason in the Jefferson County Courthouse at the corner of George and Washington Streets and hanged a month later. With his last words, Brown noted the inevitable approach of civil war, saying he was "quite certain that the crimes of this guilty land will never be purged away but with blood." A small **museum** (Mon.–Sat. 10 AM–4 PM; donations) operates in the basement of the town library, a block from the old courthouse on Washington and South Samuel Street.

South of Charles Town, US-340 winds along the western slopes of the Appalachians for a dozen miles before entering Virginia east of Winchester.

VIRGINIA

The Appalachian Trail covers more ground in Virginia than it does in any other state, following the crest of the Blue Ridge Mountains from Harpers Ferry in West Virginia all the way south to the Tennessee and North Carolina borders. In the northern half of the state, the road route closely follows the hikers' route, and the two crisscross each other through the sylvan groves of **Shenandoah National Park.** Midway along the state the two routes diverge, and hikers turn west while the motor route follows the unsurpassed Blue Ridge Parkway along the top of the world.

Most of the time the route follows the mountain crests, though in many places you'll find fascinating towns and cities a short distance to the east or west. Best among these is **Charlottesville,** a history-rich Piedmont town that's best known as the home of Thomas Jefferson and the University of Virginia. Other suggested stops include the Shenandoah Valley town of **Lexington,** the "natural wonder" of **Natural Bridge,** and the engaging city of **Roanoke.**

Dinosaur Land

Located at the intersection of US-340 and US-522, eight miles southeast of Winchester near the hamlet of White Post, **Dinosaur Land** (daily; $5; 540/869-2222) displays an entertaining and marvelously kitschy collection of man-made sharks, cavemen and, of course, dinosaurs. It's especially fun for kids, who are welcome to climb on and around the concrete menagerie, and wry-humored adults will enjoy searching through the very large gift shop, which has all manner of cheesy souvenirs.

White Post, by the way, got its name from—you guessed it—a white post, placed here by a young surveyor named George Washington. The post marked the road to the country estate of Lord Fairfax, which was destroyed in 1858.

Front Royal and Little Washington

The town of Front Royal takes its name, perhaps apocryphally, from a Revolutionary War drill sergeant who, since his troops were unable to tell their left from their right, was forced to shout out "Front Royal Oak" to get them to face the same way. **Front Royal** (pop. 13,589) sits just south of I-66 at the entrance to Shenandoah National Park. Because of its key location, Front Royal has grown unwieldy in past decades but retains some semblance of its 19th-century self along Chester Street, a well-maintained historic district at the center of town, a block east of US-340. You can also rent a boat and float along the South

Fork of the Shenandoah River, thanks to the friendly folks at the **Front Royal Canoe Company,** 8567 Stonewall Jackson Highway (540/635-5440).

At the foot of the Blue Ridge Mountains, 26 miles southeast of Front Royal via US-522, pristine, colonial **Washington** (pop. 200) was surveyed by the future father of the United States, George Washington, who named many of the streets after friends and family. The main attraction here is the **Inn at Little Washington** at Main and Middle Streets (540/675-3800), which over the past 30 years has grown from modest origins into one of the few Mobil five-star resort hotels in the country. (It has to be said that with room rates starting at over $500 a night and dinners averaging $200 a head, it's definitely a special-occasion place to stay or eat.) It's worth it, though, especially if someone else is paying the bill: A critic for *The New York Times* said his dinner there was "the most fantastic meal of my life."

Shenandoah National Park

One of the most popular national parks in the east, especially during the fall foliage season when seemingly

Housed in an old feed store off I-81 in **Middletown**, the **Route 11 Potato Chip Factory** (Mon.–Sat.; 540/869-0104), at 7815 Main Street, is said to be the smallest in the country. When it's open, you can watch the spudmasters at work and sample the freshly made chips.

everyone in the world descends upon the place to "leaf-peep," **Shenandoah National Park** protects some 300 square miles of hardwood forest along the northernmost crest of the Blue Ridge Mountains. Though the landscape looks natural now, the aboriginal forests were logged out and the landscape was heavily cultivated until the 1920s. During the Depression, when the depleted soils could no longer sustain the residents, thousands of farmers

The Blue Ridge Parkway: From Shenandoah National Park to Roanoke

Starting at the southern end of Shenandoah National Park, and winding along the crest of the Blue Ridge Mountains all the way to Great Smoky Mountains National Park some 469 miles away, the Blue Ridge Parkway is one of the country's great scenic drives. This is especially true during autumn, when the dogwoods and gum trees turn deep red, and the hickories yellow, against an evergreen backdrop of pines, hemlocks, and firs. Spring is wildflower time, with abundant azaleas and rhododendrons blooming orange, white, pink, and red throughout May and June, especially at the higher elevations.

First proposed in the 1920s, the Blue Ridge Parkway was constructed in many stages between 1935 and 1967, during which time it grew from a network of local roads to the current route, along which billboards and commercial traffic are both banned. While the Parkway avoids towns and commercial areas to concentrate on the scenery, many interesting towns and other places along the way are well worth a detour. For ease of use, we've divided the Blue Ridge Parkway into three main sections, starting with the drive between Shenandoah National Park and Roanoke. (For the Roanoke–North Carolina section, see page 93; for the final run south to the Great Smoky Mountains, see page 100.)

and their families moved out and the government began buying up the land to return it to its "natural" state.

Most people experience the park from the top, by driving along the famously beautiful Skyline Drive. This road climbs up from the Shenandoah Valley but mostly runs along the crest, offering grand vistas (when the air is clear, at least). Besides the hardwood forests, the park also protects numerous waterfalls, wildflower meadows, and understory plants like azaleas

Along with multicolored leaves, the autumn months bring hundreds of hawks, eagles, and other birds of prey to the mountains on their annual migration. You'll spot the greatest numbers of raptors in late September.

Mile 0: Rockfish Gap, at the southern end of Shenandoah National Park's Skyline Drive, marks the northern start of the Blue Ridge Parkway.

Milepost 6.1: Humpback Rocks has a short but strenuous trail (45 minutes each way), leading through a reconstructed farmstead and a visitors center (540/943-4716), ending with a 270-degree view over the mountains.

Milepost 34.4: Yankee Horse parking area has an exhibit on an old logging railroad, part of which has been restored, and a short trail to Wigwam Falls.

Milepost 63.6: James River Visitor Center (804/299-5496), exhibits, and trails along the James River and Kanawha Canal. This is the lowest point on the Parkway, at 649 feet, and also the junction with US-501, which runs west along the James River for 15 miles to Natural Bridge.

Milepost 76.5: Great views over both valleys from the highest point on the Parkway in Virginia, at 3,950 feet.

Milepost 84–87: The most popular—and most developed—stretch of the Parkway, the Peaks of Otter section includes a visitors center, gas station, restaurant, and very pleasant lodge ($60–90; 540/586-1081), open year-round. Three peaks rise above a small lake and give great sunrise and sunset views; many good trails, including a two-mile loop to Fallingwater Cascades, let you escape the sometimes-sizeable crowds.

Milepost 105: The city of Roanoke.

Skyline Drive

Most people experience Shenandoah National Park by driving the spectacular Skyline Drive. The drive, which was plotted and surveyed in 1931 and opened in 1939, runs (at 35 mph!) along the crest over 100 miles, winding between the I-66 and I-64 freeways while giving grand vistas at every bend in the road. Mileposts, arranged in mile-by-mile order from north to south, mark your progress along Skyline Drive. The scenic driving is definitely memorable, but by far the best way to really see the park is to get out of the car and walk along the many miles of trails (including more than 100 miles of the Appalachian Trail) that lead through the dense green forests to innumerable waterfalls and overlooks.

A helpful map and brochure is handed out at entrance booths along the route (one at either end and two midway). Here are some more great places to look out for:

Milepost 21.1: Roadside parking area marks the trailhead for a lovely, 3.2 mile hike to Overall Run Falls, the tallest in the park. You can also reach the falls from Matthews Arm campground, just down the road.

Milepost 31.5: Thornton Gap, the junction with US-211.

Milepost 32.4: Mary's Rock Tunnel, a 670-foot-long, 13-foot-wide bore cut through the granite in 1932.

and mountain laurels, which bloom brightest in late spring. There is considerable development in the park, with a pair of rustic lodges and enough gas stations and restaurants and campgrounds to handle the thousands of visitors who flock (especially in October, for the autumn foliage). Despite the crowds, it's not hard to find peace and quiet, especially if you venture off on even the briefest of hikes.

There is a ranger station at each entrance to the park, where you pay your $10 per-car fee (or show your pass). There's a **visitors center** (540/999-3500) at each end of Skyline Drive, and one in the middle, at Big Meadows (milepost 51). Trails at Big Meadows lead past herds of very tame deer to Dark Hollow Falls, which drops 70 feet over

Milepost 50.7: Near Big Meadows, under a mile from the well-marked trailhead, Dark Hollow Falls tumbles over a 70-foot incline. Outside the Byrd Visitor Center, a macho statue of "Iron Mike" commemorates the efforts of the workers who built the trails, overlooks, and campgrounds as part of the New Deal Civilian Conservation Corps.

Milepost 52.8: Milan Gap marks the start of a two-mile walk to Rapidan Camp, where President Hoover established a trout-fishing retreat in 1929.

Milepost 56.4: A short, steep hike scrambles up to the 3,300-foot-high summit of Bearfence Mountain for a 360-degree panorama.

Milepost 84.1: A parking area marks the trailhead for the rewarding 3.6-mile hike to Jones Run Falls, tumbling over a mossy 45-foot cliff.

Milepost 98.9: Near the southern end of Skyline Drive, Calf Mountain provides a grand panorama over the Shenandoah Valley.

greenish volcanic stone. The Big Meadows Lodge was built in 1939 and retains its cozy feel; this is also where the park's largest campground is located. There's another lodge to the north, at Skyland (milepost 42), the highest point on Skyline Drive. There are full-service restaurants at both lodges; all food and lodging (and most everything else in the park) is managed by a private concession, Aramark (540/743-5108).

Luray Caverns

Halfway through Shenandoah National Park, US-211 runs west down to **Luray Caverns** (daily; $21 adults, $10 children; 540/743-6551), the largest and most impressive of the many

Detour: Charlottesville

From the southern end of Shenandoah National Park, it's a quick 20 miles east on I-64 to **Charlottesville** (pop. 45,049), a richly historic college town that's one of the most enjoyable stops in the state. From the rolling green lawns of the University of Virginia campus to neoclassical Monticello on the hills above it, the legacy of Thomas Jefferson dominates Charlottesville. Jefferson lived and worked here for most of his life—when he wasn't out founding the country or serving as its president.

West of the compact downtown district, the **University of Virginia** campus was Jefferson's pride and joy. Not only did he found it (in 1819) and fund its early years, he planned the curriculum and designed the original buildings, a quadrangle of redbrick Palladian villas that the American Institute of Architects declared the most perfect place in the country. Edgar Allan Poe lived and studied here briefly before dropping out in 1826. Poe's room, appropriately, is No. 13 in the West Range, and it's decorated to look like it did a century ago, with a few period belongings visible behind the glass door. When school is in session, free campus tours are offered five times a day by the **University Guides** (434/924-3239).

Charlottesville's other key sight is Jefferson's home, **Monticello**—the domed building that fills the back of the nickel coin—well signed off I-64, exit 121. Recently restored and open for tours (daily; $20; 434/984-9822), Monticello embodies the many different traits of this multifaceted man. The house was designed and built by Jefferson over a period of 40 years (1769–1809) and holds various gadgets he invented—including a double-pen device that made a copy of everything he wrote—and odd things he

Monticello, home of Thomas Jefferson

collected over the years, from elk antlers to recipes for home-brewed beer. Jefferson died here at Monticello on July 4, 1826, and the grounds, which in Jefferson's time formed an extensive plantation worked by slaves, hold his mortal remains in a simple tomb beyond the vegetable gardens.

Down in the valley below Monticello, **Michie Tavern** (daily; $8 adults, $3 children; 434/977-1234) is a touristy but interesting inn that opened in 1784 and was moved to the present site in the 1920s. Admission includes a tour of the parlors, bars, and upstairs rooms, as well as a dairy and a gristmill. Michie Tavern is also a restaurant serving "Olde Worlde foode" for the bus-tour hordes, at $18 a head (plus dessert!) for a "colonial buffet" lunch. (Just so you know, Michie is pronounced MICK-ee, as in Mantle.)

Practicalities

Like most college towns, Charlottesville provides a broad range of good places to eat, from bare-bones cafés like the **White Spot** (434/295-9899), right across from campus at 1407 University Avenue—this is the place to satisfy those midnight cravings for a cheeseburger with a fried egg on top, known here as a "Gus Burger." On the downtown "Mall" you'll find places like **Rapture** (434/293-9526) at 303 E. Main Street, which offers eclectic Asian dishes alongside steaks and fish-and-chips. It's also a very popular nightclub, with pool tables, dancing, and a modish bar. Also on the Mall, try the modish versions of diner food at **Bizou,** 119 W. Main Street (434/977-1818), and there's more great live music at **Miller's** (434/971-8511) at 109 W. Main Street, where alt-rock pop star Dave Matthews used to tend bar. For great barbecued ribs and chicken, head over to **Jinx's Pit Stop,** 1307 E. Market Street (434/293-6904).

Most of Charlottesville's motels line up along Emmett Street (US-29 Business), near the US-250 freeway, including the well-placed **English Inn** at 2000 Morton Drive ($90 and up; 434/971-9000). For more detailed information on visiting Charlottesville, contact the **visitors center** (434/293-6789 or 877/386-1102), which is hard to miss along I-64 at exit 121.

Fall foliage in the Blue Ridge Mountains can be stunning, though it is not usually as intense as in New England.

Pollution from metropolitan areas and from so many car-borne visitors has caused serious problems at Shenandoah National Park, both for the trees—many of which have been poisoned—and for the views people come to see. On an average summer day, visibility is impaired and the surrounding valleys are often shrouded in smoggy haze.

caverns in the limestone Blue Ridge region—a single room measures 300 by 500 feet and is over 140 feet high. It also boasts the "World's Only Stalacpipe Organ," where rubber mallets make music by banging on the stone stalactites. There's also a large antique car museum and a garden maze (included in caverns admission).

Near the caverns, along US-211 a half mile west of town, the **Luray Zoo** (daily; $8; 540/743-4113) is an animal rescue center and zoo that's home to one of Virginia's largest collections of scaly creatures, both extinct and living. Cobras, alligators, and 20-foot pythons coexist with tropical birds, big cats, and cheerful, playful monkeys. For younger children, there's also a petting zoo of goats, deer, donkeys, pigs, and all manner of farmyard animals.

Staunton

West of the mountains from the south end of Shenandoah National Park on I-64, tidy **Staunton** (pop. 23,853; STAN-ton) was founded in 1732 as one of the first towns on the far side of the Blue Ridge. Unlike much of the valley, Staunton was untouched during the Civil War and now preserves its many 18th- and early 19th-century buildings in a townscape so perfect it was rated among the dozen most distinctive destinations in the United States by the National Trust for Historic Preservation.

One of Staunton's many sizable historic districts surrounds the boyhood home of favorite son Woodrow Wilson. Son of a Presbyterian minister, Wilson was born in 1856 in a stately Greek Revival townhouse at 18–24 N. Coalter Street, now established as the **Woodrow Wilson Birthplace and Museum** (daily; $12; 540/885-0897), with galleries tracing

Woodrow Wilson

his life as a scholar—he was president of Princeton University—and as U.S. President during World War I.

Staunton is also the home of the unique **Frontier Culture Museum** (daily; $10; 540/332-7850), right off I-81 exit 222 on the east side of town. A rural version of Williamsburg, this living history museum consists of four resurrected working farms, incorporating buildings brought over from Germany, England, and Ireland. The fourth farm, dating from antebellum Virginia, shows how various "Old World" traditions blended in America. The farms are inhabited by interpreters dressed in (very clean) period costumes busily husking corn, spinning wool, or working in the fields.

Staunton holds one of the best places to eat in the Shenandoah Valley, on US-250 just east of I-81 exit 222, near the frontier museum: **Mrs. Rowe's Family Restaurant** (540/886-1833), which has been serving excellent, home-style cooking, from pork chops to banana cream pies, for the past 60 years. It's open every day (since 1947) for breakfast, lunch, and dinner—go for the world-famous fried chicken, which is well worth the 25-minute wait. Staunton is also home to another classic: **Wright's Dairy-Rite** (540/886-0435), at 346 Greenville Avenue, with great burgers, hot dogs, and onion rings, served up in your car or a dining room decorated with old menus. Enjoy free Wi-Fi, and a free Wurlitzer jukebox.

If you've had enough road food and junk food, try the locally sourced produce and other fine foods at the **Staunton Grocery,** in the heart of downtown at 105 W. Beverley Street (540/886-6880).

All the usual motels cluster around the

Just east of the Skyline Drive, three miles northeast of I-64 exit 107, "Virginia's Best Pizza" has been served up for more than 25 years inside barn-red **Crozet Pizza** (434/823-2132) on Hwy-240 at 5794 Three Notched Road.

Earl Hamner Jr. based his famous 1970s TV series *The Waltons* on vivid memories of growing up during the Depression in the rural village of Schuyler, a half hour southwest of Charlottesville. Fans of the show will enjoy visiting the **Walton's Mountain Museum** (Mar.–Nov. daily; $6; 434/831-2000), which re-creates the Waltons' kitchen and living room (and John-Boy's bedroom) in the Schuyler Community Center—Earle Hamner's old elementary school.

While in Staunton, check out the wares available at the **Jolly Roger Haggle Shop,** a fascinating junk shop ("over 1,000,000 items") across from the train station at 27 Middlebrook Avenue.

I-64/I-81 junction, but you'll find the region's most pleasant accommodations at the rambling Victorian-era **Belle Grae Inn** ($100 and up; 540/886-5151), at 515 W. Frederick Street in the center of Staunton, with B&B rooms, a lovely garden, and a fine restaurant.

Lexington

Founded in 1778, and named for the then-recent Revolutionary War battleground, photogenic **Lexington** (pop. 6,959) is home to an estimable pair of Virginia institutions, the Virginia Military Institute (VMI) and Washington and Lee University, which meld into one another at the center of town. Numerous old brick buildings, including a typically southern lawyer's row around Courthouse Square, still stand around the town, which you can tour on foot or in one of the horse-drawn carriages that leave from the downtown visitors center.

Animated by an unusually crew-cut version of typical college-town energy, Lexington is redolent with, and intensely proud of, its military heritage. Generals, in fact, have become the town's stock-in-trade: From 1859 until his death in 1863, **Gen. Thomas "Stonewall" Jackson** lived at 8 E. Washington Street, now a small **museum** (daily; $6; 540/463-2552); he is buried in the small but well-tended cemetery a short distance west of downtown. Gen. Robert E. Lee spent his post–Civil War years teaching at Washington and Lee, which was named after him (and his wife's ancestor George). Lee is entombed in a crypt below the chapel, under a famous statue of his recumbent self, with his trusty horse, Traveller, buried just outside. Another influential old warhorse, Gen. George C. Marshall, is honored in a large eponymous museum (daily; $3) on the VMI campus. The museum traces General Marshall's role in planning the D-Day invasions in World War II and salutes his Nobel Peace Prize–winning "Marshall Plan" for the successful reconstruction of postwar Europe.

Spend a summer night in Lexington at the community-run **Hull's Drive In** (540/463-2621), at 2367 N. US-11, a much-loved local Ozoner drive-in theater still showing Hollywood hits.

To get a sense of life in the Shenandoah Valley, tune to **WSVA 550 AM** in Harrisonburg, which broadcasts updated farm and livestock prices every hour on the hour.

There are a number of comfortable and captivating places to stay in and around Lexington, like the **Llewellyn Lodge** ($79–195; 540/463-3235 or

800/882-1145) at 603 S. Main Street. Comfortable, convenient, welcoming, and helpful, and within easy walking distance of the campuses and the historic town center, the Llewellyn is everything a B&B should be.

Natural Bridge

Held sacred by local Monacan Indians and bought from King George in 1774 by Thomas Jefferson, the 215-foot-high notch of Natural Bridge is a remarkable piece of geologic acrobatics. Spanning some 90 feet, the thick stone arch bridges Cedar Creek at the bottom of a steeply walled canyon. To see the Natural Bridge, which is heralded as one of the Seven Natural Wonders of the World (others on the list include Niagara Falls, Yellowstone, and Giant's Causeway in Northern Ireland), you have  to buy a ticket (daily; $18; 800/533-1410) from the unbelievably huge souvenir shop that fills the bottom of the old hotel. Natural Bridge is the focus of a once-plush resort complex that has definitely seen better times but still offers some 200 rooms in two hotels, as well as a large cave and a wax museum of Virginia history in which you can watch the wax figures being made, dressed, and posed.

The **Natural Bridge Inn,** located next to the Natural Bridge entrance, has rooms ($75 and up) and four- to six-room cottages across the road for a little more. There's also an Olympic-sized pool, and the colonial dining room serves all meals daily, with outdoor dining on the veranda and popular weekend buffets.

Roanoke

Apart from Asheville at its southern end, **Roanoke** (pop. 94,911) is the only real city that can claim it's actually *on* the Blue Ridge Parkway. With block after block of brick-fronted business buildings, most of them adorned with neon, metal, and painted signs that seem unchanged since the 1940s, Roanoke contrasts abruptly with the natural verdancy of the

For NPR news and non-commercial arts programming, tune to **WVTF 89.1 FM** in Roanoke.

rest of the Parkway, but you may find it a welcome change after so many trees. Once a busy, belching, industrial Goliath supported by the railroads, Roanoke has evolved into a sophisticated, high-tech city—the commercial, cultural, and medical center of southwest Virginia.

Roanoke's main visitor attractions lie right downtown in the **Center in the Square** complex (540/342-5700), a restored warehouse that holds a wide variety of cultural offerings, including theaters, an art museum (free), a kid-friendly science museum ($6), and a local history museum ($3). Also worth a look is the **Virginia Museum of Transportation** (daily; $8; 540/342-5670), three blocks west of Center in the Square at 303 Norfolk Avenue, which displays lots of old cars and trucks, steam and diesel locomotives, and horse-drawn carriages, plus a complete traveling circus—minus the performers, of course. Steam trains, as documented by Roanoke-based photographer O. Winston Link, are the real highlight of the museum, and a short walk away at 101 Shenandoah Avenue, inside Roanoke's streamlined 1930s-era Norfolk & Western Railroad passenger station, the new **O. Winston Link Museum** (daily; $5; 540/982-LINK) displays more than 200 of the photographer's indelible black-and-white images. There's also a neat gallery devoted to the building's legendary designer, Raymond Loewy, who created the Coke bottle, the logo for Lucky Strike cigarettes, and hundreds of other all-American icons.

On Mill Mountain high above Roanoke, the 100-foot-tall **"World's Largest Man-Made Star"** shines nightly, lit by 2,000 feet of red, white and blue neon tubing. You can drive up to the base of it and get a grand view over Roanoke.

"World's Largest Man-Made Star," on Roanoke's Mill Mountain

Roanoke Practicalities

Roanoke's most popular place to eat is **The Roanoker** (540/344-7746), "The Home of Good Food since

1941," which serves traditional Virginia dishes and also does a tasty bowl of chili, a mile south of downtown off I-581 (Wonju Street exit) at 2522 Colonial Avenue. There are also a number of good cafés downtown, plus the unexpected world-beat cuisine at **Carlos' Brazilian and International Cuisine** (540/776-1117) on a hilltop three miles south of town at 4167 Electric Road. If you're planning a picnic up in the mountains, be sure to stop first at the historic **farmers market** (closed Sun.; free), downtown next to the Center in the Square and active since 1874.

In the mountains west of Roanoke, across I-81 on Hwy-311 in Catawba, excellent home cooking ($15 for all you can eat: fresh biscuits, fried chicken, incredible fresh fruit cobblers) is served Thursday–Sunday, for dinner only, at **The Home Place** (540/384-7252).

Places to stay range from the usual Interstate motels, lined up along Orange Avenue (US-460), to a pair of grand hotels. Oldest and best of these is the **Hotel Roanoke** ($120 and up; 540/985-5900 or 800/222-8733), at 110 Shenandoah Avenue, which has anchored downtown for over a century. Now managed as a Doubletree, the hotel has outlasted the railroads that financed it, and even if you stay elsewhere, the lobby, with its Florentine marble floors and vaulted ceiling, is worth a look.

Southeast of Roanoke, the **Booker T. Washington National Monument** (540/721-2094) preserves the tobacco fields and plantation cabin where the influential African American leader was born. Other buildings on the 225-acre site, 20 miles from Roanoke via Hwy-116 and Hwy-122, have been reconstructed.

The soft drink **Dr. Pepper,** which originated in Waco, Texas, was named for a pharmacist who worked in the town of **Rural Retreat,** Virginia, along I-81 near its intersection with the AT.

Floyd

The town of **Floyd,** west of the Blue Ridge Parkway, about an hour southwest of Roanoke, has only one stoplight, so it's easy to find the **Floyd Country Store,** which is famous for its weekly Jamboree ($3; 540/745-4563). Every Friday at 7 PM, the display cases are pushed aside and the floor given over to *real* country music and shuffling feet.

NORTH CAROLINA

Running along the crest of the Blue Ridge Mountains at the far western edge of the state, this route across North Carolina takes in some of the most beautiful scenery east or west of the Mississippi. Though not as immense as the Rockies or other western landscapes, this part of North Carolina abounds with rugged peaks and deep valleys, pastoral meadows, and ancient-looking mountain villages, some dating back to colonial times. It's all linked by the magnificent Blue Ridge Parkway, perhaps the country's greatest scenic drive.

The region's sole city, **Asheville,** is a proud old resort dominated by the ostentatious Biltmore Estate, the world's largest private house, but everywhere else nature predominates—especially in the majestic **Great Smoky Mountains National Park** in the state's far southwestern corner.

Mount Airy: Mayberry, RFD

Along the Virginia/North Carolina border, 12 miles southeast of Blue Ridge Parkway milepost 200 via US-52, **Mount Airy** (pop. 7,156) was the boyhood home of Andy Griffith, who based much of his long-running TV show *The Andy Griffith Show* and the spin-off sitcom *Mayberry, RFD* on the region. If you have fond memories of Opie, Andy, Barney, and Aunt Bee, you'll definitely want to visit Mount Airy, which has effectively re-created itself in the image of the show. Take a "squad car" tour (336/789-OPIE) and let a wannabe Barney show you the sights. Eat an ever-tender pork chop sandwich, raved about by *Gourmet Magazine* and Oprah, at the very popular **Snappy Lunch** (closed Sun.; 336/786-4931), at 125 Main Street in the compact downtown business district. And don't neglect to admire the 8x10

In the valley below Mount Mitchell, off I-40 northeast of Asheville, **Black Mountain College** was a lively intellectual and artistic nexus during the 1930s and 1940s.

Mount Airy is home to the world's largest open-face granite quarry.

the sheriff's car, parked outside Mayberry Motor Inn

The Blue Ridge Parkway: Roanoke to North Carolina

South from Roanoke, the Blue Ridge Parkway winds another 100 miles before crossing the North Carolina border. This midsection of the Parkway, especially the first 25 miles south of Roanoke, runs at a lower elevation across a more settled and cultivated landscape than the rugged ridge tops followed elsewhere. In place of the spectacular vistas, you'll see many more houses and small farms, a few pioneer cabins (preserved and not), miles of split-rail fences, and some picturesque cemeteries. The southern reaches, approaching the North Carolina border, get better and better.

Milepost 122: The city of Roanoke.

Milepost 154.5: A two-mile loop trail leads to a pioneer cabin overlooking the Smart View for which it's named. Blooming dogwoods abound in May.

Milepost 165.2: At Tuggles Gap, the junction with Hwy-8 has a motel, restaurant, gas station, and also a small cemetery right along the Parkway.

Mileposts 167–174: The 4,800-acre Rocky Knob area contains a campground (540/745-9662), a visitors center near the Meadows of Dan, and a strenuous but very rewarding 10-mile roundtrip trail (starting at MP 167.1) leading down through Rock Castle Gorge and over 3,572-foot Rocky Knob.

Milepost 176.1: A short trail leads to Mabry Mill, in use 1910–1935. In summer, interpreters demonstrate blacksmithing and milling skills. A coffee shop (open May–Oct. only) sells old-fashioned pancakes made from stone-ground flour, plus country ham and hamburgers.

Milepost 199–200: Junction with US-52, which runs south to Mount Airy, North Carolina, home of Mayberry, RFD.

Milepost 216.9: Virginia/North Carolina border.

glossies of Mayberry actors and their local lookalikes at Floyd's Barber Shop, next door. Or head a few blocks west to **Aunt Bea's Barbeque,** 425 Old US-52 (336/789-3050). Then stay the night at the comfortable, clean, and inexpensive **Mayberry Motor Inn** ($50 and up; 336/786-4109) across the highway—just look for the black-and-white Mayberry sheriff's car parked out front.

The Mayberry mania reaches a peak during **Mayberry Days** in late September; details on this (and anything to do with Andy Griffith) can be had from the **Mount Airy visitors center** (800/948-0949).

Blowing Rock

A quick two miles south of the Blue Ridge Parkway via US-221 from milepost 291.9 lies the delightful little resort community of **Blowing Rock** (pop. 1,418)—the place to stop if you're only stopping once. The cool summer temperatures have been attracting visitors

for centuries, and once you get past the factory outlet mall that welcomes you to town, quaint old Main Street is a great place to stretch your legs while taking in the eclectic range of late Victorian buildings, including some delightful churches. Blowing Rock takes its name from a nearby cliff overlooking John's River Gorge, where updrafts can cause lightweight objects to be blown upwards rather than down; this effect, which earned Blowing Rock a mention in *Ripley's Believe It or Not!* as the only place "Where Snow Falls Upside Down," also inspired the Native American legend of a Cherokee brave who, rather than be forcibly separated from his Chickasaw lover, leapt off the cliff, only to be blown back into the arms of his sweetheart.

North Carolina's oldest tourist attraction, the **Blowing Rock** itself, two miles east of town via winding US-321 (daily; $6), is worth the admission, whether or not the "magic wind" is blowing. Check out the tremendous views from a platform suspended 3,000 feet above the valley below. The nearby area also offers a couple of enjoyable tourist traps, including an apparently gravity-defying **"Mystery Hill"** just off the Parkway, and the toddler-friendly, coal-fired steam trains of the **Tweetsie Railroad,** four miles north of town on US-321.

Downtown Blowing Rock has a number of good places to eat lined up along and around the quaint few blocks of Main Street downtown, like **Crippen's Country Inn,** 239 Sunset Drive (828/295-3487). Across US-321 from the Blowing Rock, the storybook **Green Park Inn** ($100–150; 828/295-3141) is a large historic resort hotel built in 1882, with a golf course. More modern conveniences are available at the **Cliff Dwellers Inn** ($80 and up; 828/295-3121), right off the parkway on US-321.

Little Switzerland

Another classic mountaintop vacation spot, located midway between Blowing Rock and Asheville, Little Switzerland was founded in 1910 around the **Switzerland Inn** ($125 and up; 828/765-2153 or 800/654-4026), a peaceful and relaxing old chalet-style resort that also operates a very popular restaurant right off the Blue Ridge Parkway at milepost 334.

The inn stands on a crest, but the rest of Little Switzerland sits in the deep canyon to the east, spread out along Hwy-226 and a number of smaller side roads. The main stop is **Emerald Village** (daily April–Nov.; $5; 828/765-6463), on McKinney

Mine Road 2.5 miles from the Parkway, where you can tour an old gemstone mine (above and below ground) and museums displaying everything from gemstones to mechanical music makers.

Asheville

What the English country town of Bath was to Jane Austen's 18-century London, the mountain resort of **Asheville** (pop. 68,889) was to the pre–jet set, pre–air-conditioned Deep South. When summer heat and humidity became unbearable, the gentry headed here to stay cool while enjoying the city's many grand hotels and elaborate summer homes.

The hikers' Appalachian Trail winds west of the Blue Ridge Parkway along the North Carolina/ Tennessee border.

The presence here of the world's biggest vacation house, the Vanderbilt family's **Biltmore Estate** (daily; $60; 800/543-2961), is proof of Asheville's primary position in the old-school resort pantheon. The estate now covers 8,000 acres on the south side of town, though at the turn of the twentieth century it covered more than 100,000 acres, stretching all the way up to today's Blue Ridge Parkway. Surrounded by a series of flower gardens planned in part by Frederick Law Olmsted, the estate centers on a truly unbelievable French Renaissance–style mansion built in 1895. The 250-plus rooms hold everything from a palm court and a bowling alley to Napoleon's chess set to paintings by Renoir, Singer Sargent, Whistler, and others. Signs aplenty direct you to the estate, which stands just north of the I-40 exit 50 off Biltmore Avenue, across from the shops and restaurants in **Historic Biltmore Village,** which originally housed the estate's staff and workshops—it's a true "model village," designed in gothic style by Richard Morris Hunt.

Asheville's long-standing relationship with visitors explains why the local minor league baseball team is called the **Asheville Tourists.** The Colorado Rockies farm club plays at retro-modern McCormick Field, a mile south of downtown (828/258-0428). Games are broadcast on **WRES 100.7 FM.**

The rest of Asheville can't compete with the nouveau riche excess of the Biltmore Estate, and in fact it's a surprisingly homespun city, with a downtown commercial district filled with 1930s-era storefronts housing thrift stores and offbeat art galleries. One truly worthwhile place to see in downtown Asheville is the nondescript old boardinghouse where author Thomas Wolfe grew up from 1900 to 1920, preserved as it was when

For good commercial-free music and NPR news in and around Asheville, tune to **WNCW 88.7 FM.**

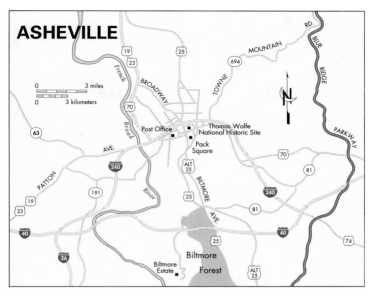

Wolfe lived here. The rambling house, at 48 Spruce Street across from the beige modern Radisson Hotel, is officially known as the **Thomas Wolfe Memorial State Historic Site** (daily, closed Mon. in winter; $1; 828/253-8304); unfortunately, the house suffered a major fire in 1998, but after restoration is still one of the most evocative of all American literary sites. In the details and, more impor-

A dozen miles west of the Blue Ridge Parkway via US-321 and Hwy-194, the village of Valle Crucis holds the original **Mast General Store,** a one-of-a-kind survivor that sells a little of everything, from gasoline to Gore-Tex parkas. There is now a branch in Blowing Rock.

tantly, in general ambience, it's identical to the vivid prose descriptions of the house he called "Dixieland," the primary setting of his first and greatest novel, *Look Homeward, Angel.* After Wolfe's death from tuberculosis in 1938, the house was made into a shrine to Wolfe by his family, who arranged it to look as it did during his youth; one room contains his desk, typewriter, and other mementos of his life and work. An adjacent museum tells more of his story.

Two blocks south of the Wolfe memorial, where Broadway becomes Biltmore Avenue, **Pack Square** is the center of Asheville, surrounded by the county courthouse, the city hall, a small art museum, and the public library. This is where Thomas Wolfe's father ran a stonecutting shop, on whose porch stood the homeward-gazing angel, now recalled by a statue standing on the square's southwest corner.

Asheville Practicalities

The streets around Pack Square hold many good places to eat, including a trio of bistro-type places with outdoor dining areas, lined up side by side around the **Bistro 1896** (828/251-1300), at 7 SW. Pack Square. There are more good places around the magical, art deco–era Grove shopping arcade west of the square, and yet more cafés and bakeries line Biltmore Avenue south of Pack Square, where you'll also find Asheville's best nightlife. The **Orange Peel** (828/255-5851), at

Profits from Grove's Tasteless Tonic paid for the ultra-tasteful Grove Park Inn.

101 S. Biltmore Avenue, gets an enviable array of nationally known musicians in all genres (from Bob Dylan to the Flaming Lips) while the **Fine Arts cinema** across the street shows the latest art-house releases. North of downtown, near the UNC-Asheville campus, good microbrews (and $3 evening movies) are available at **Asheville Pizza and Brewing,** 675 Merrimon Avenue (828/254-1281).

Novelist **F. Scott Fitzgerald** stayed at Asheville's Grove Park Resort while visiting his wife, **Zelda,** who had been committed to the adjacent Highland Hospital sanitarium, where she died in a fire in 1948.

Twenty miles southwest of Asheville, the eponymous peak featured in the book *Cold Mountain* rises amidst the Pisgah National Forest, but the Academy Award–winning movie version was filmed on location—in distant Romania.

The usual chain hotels cluster along the Interstates, and some more characterful older, neon-signed motels line old US-70 between downtown and the Blue Ridge Parkway. For a true taste of Americana, you may prefer the classic 1930s **Log Cabin Motor Court** ($50–85; 828/645-6546), six miles north of Asheville at 330 Weaverville Highway. To complete the retro experience, there's a roller-skating rink next door.

When Vanderbilt types come to Asheville today, they probably stay at **Grove Park Inn Resort** ($250 and up; 828/252-2711 or 800/438-0050), at 290 Macon Avenue north of I-90, a lovely rustic inn built in 1913. Newer wings contain the most modern four-star conveniences, but the original lodge boasts rooms filled with authentic Roycroft furniture, making the Grove Park a live-in museum of arts-and-crafts style. There's also a very plush **Inn on Biltmore Estate** ($190 and up; 828/225-1600), for the full Biltmore Estate experience.

For further information on the Asheville area, contact the **visitors center** (828/258-6101 or 800/257-1300), at 151 Haywood Street off I-240 exit 4C.

You can spot the wild mountains southeast of Asheville in numerous movies including *Last of the Mohicans,* much of which was filmed around Chimney Rock, east of town along scenic US-64. **Chimney Rock** (800/277-9611) is a great destination, featuring fabulous views and a 26-story elevator carved through solid granite.

Maggie Valley

The Blue Ridge Parkway swings south from Asheville through Transylvania County on the approach to Great Smoky Mountains National Park, though you'll save an hour or more by following the I-40 freeway to the junction with US-19, which links up with the south end of the parkway. This stretch of US-19, winding through the Maggie Valley over the foothills of the Great Smokies, is a very pretty drive, and absolutely packed with roadside Americana—miniature golf courses, trout farms, souvenir shops, lookout towers alongside pancake houses, barbecue shacks…you name it, it's here.

For years, the biggest and best of many great places to stop in Maggie Valley has been **Ghost Town in the Sky,** a real, old Appalachian ghost town–themed amusement park (May–Sept. daily; $30; 828/926-1140), with roller coasters, bumper cars, and all the usual suspects, high on the side of the Great Smoky Mountains. Built in the 1960's, the park has been plagued by financial problems in recent years. Call to see if they're open, then hop on the chairlift or funicular up the mountain, and have some fun.

Cherokee

West of Maggie Valley, the Blue Ridge Parkway and US-19

The Blue Ridge Parkway: North Carolina to the Smokies

The highest and most memorable parts of the 469-mile Blue Ridge Parkway are the 250 mountainous miles leading along the backbone of North Carolina. Following the southern Blue Ridge Mountains as they fade into the taller and more massive Black Mountains, the Parkway skirts three other mountain ranges before ending up at Great Smoky Mountains National Park on the Tennessee border. Spring flowers (including massive rhododendrons), fall colors, songbirds, wild turkeys, numerous waterfalls, and occasional eerie fogs that fill the valleys below all make this an unforgettable trip no matter what the time of year. Take your time and drive carefully, however hard it is to keep your eyes on the road.

A couple of worthwhile detours—to the mountain hamlets of Blowing Rock and Little Switzerland, and to the city of Asheville—are covered in greater detail in the main text. From north to south, here are the mile-by-mile highlights along the North Carolina portion of the Blue Ridge Parkway:

Milepost 216.9: Virginia/North Carolina border.

Milepost 217.5: A very easy half-mile trail leads to the top of 2,885-foot Cumberland Knob. A visitors center marks the location workers began construction of the parkway in 1935.

Mileposts 238.5–244.7: Doughton Park, named for one of the politicians who made the Parkway possible, is home to **Bluffs Lodge** (336/372-4499), which has nice rooms, a café serving down-home country cooking, a gas station, and a campground.

Milepost 260.6: An easy mile-long trail leads to the top of Jumpinoff Rocks for a sweeping view.

Mileposts 292–295: Moses H. Cone Memorial Park is a 3,600-acre former private estate, with many miles of mountaintop hiking trails. At Mile 294, Southern Highlands Crafts Guild members demonstrate various Appalachian crafts throughout the summer, on the front porch of the former Cone mansion, which is now the nonprofit Parkway Craft Center.

Milepost 304: The marvelous engineering feat of the Linn Cove Viaduct carries the Parkway around rugged Grandfather Mountain. Completed in 1987, this was the last part of the Parkway to be built. Dense walls of rhododendrons border the Parkway south of the viaduct.

Milepost 305.1: US-221, which used to carry the Parkway before the viaduct was built, leads a mile south to 5,837-foot **Grandfather Mountain,** the highest peak in Blue Ridge, now a private park (daily; $14; 800/468-7325) with nature trails, a zoo, and the famous "Mile-High Swinging Bridge."

Milepost 308.2: A half-mile nature trail leads to 3,995-foot Flat Rock for a view of Grandfather Mountain.

Milepost 316.3: Linville Falls crashes through a rugged gorge; short trails lead to scenic overlooks.

Milepost 331: At the junction of Hwy-226, the **Museum of North Carolina Minerals** (daily 9 AM–5 PM; free) displays all kinds and sizes of local gemstones, which you can watch being polished.

Milepost 355.4: West of the Parkway, the 1,650 acres of Mount Mitchell State Park include a mountaintop observation tower. Drive to within 200 yards of the weather-beaten 6,684-foot summit, the highest point east of the Mississippi River.

Milepost 364.6: Best seen in late spring when the rhododendrons are in full bloom, the lush greenery of Craggy Gardens feels like an Appalachian Shangri-La.

Milepost 382: You can check out exhibits and demonstrations of Appalachian arts and crafts in the Folk Art Center.

Milepost 431: At the highest point on the Parkway (6,047 feet in elevation), a self-guided nature trail leads through a first-growth spruce and fir forest.

Milepost 469: Southern end of Blue Ridge Parkway, at the junction with US-441 and the entrance to Smoky Mountains National Park.

Spending more than 50 years as a living roadside landmark, **Cherokee Chief Henry Lambert** was known as "The World's Most Photographed Indian." Though Chief Henry died in 2007, his image still graces countless Cherokee postcards.

join up 40 miles west of Asheville at touristy **Cherokee** (pop. 5,971), commercial center of the 56,000-acre **Cherokee Indian Reservation,** which was established here by a small band of Cherokee Indians in 1866, long after the rest of this once-mighty tribe had been forcibly exiled to Oklahoma on the Trail of Tears. Cherokee is a last gasp of commercialism at the edge of the national park, a traffic-clogged gauntlet of places where you can See Live Bears, Eat Boiled Peanuts, Pan For Gold, or ride the "Rudicoaster" at the kid-friendly Santa's Land amusement park. The biggest draw hereabouts is the ever-expanding Harrah's Casino.

The upscale casino, the region's biggest draw, looms over a fading roadside lined by tacky old-time souvenir stands like the "Big Chief," but amidst the tourist-taunting sprawl is at least one worthwhile stop: the **Museum of the Cherokee Indian** (daily; $9), which traces tribal history from pre-conquest achievements—the Cherokee used a natural version of aspirin centuries before western chemists "discovered" it, for example—to their forced removal after gold was discovered here in the 1830s.

Great Smoky Mountains National Park

The most popular park in the United States, **Great Smoky Mountains National Park** offers a taste of wilderness to some nine million visitors annually. Knoxville, Nashville, and Atlanta are all within a two-hour drive, and day-trippers visit

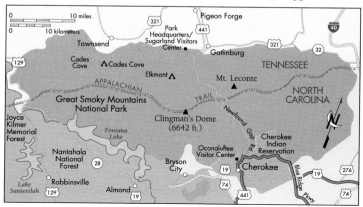

mostly during late October for the annual display of fall color. The park covers 520,460 acres along the 6,000-foot-high crest of the Great Smoky Mountains, so named for the fogs that fill the deep valleys. Before the park was established, its lands were extensively logged—70 percent of the trees had been clear-cut by 1934, when the lands were protected as a national park. Fortunately, the forests have grown back to obscure any sign of past degradations, and the uncut portions form the most extensive stands of primeval forest in the eastern United States.

The main route through the park is Newfound Gap Road (US-441), which runs northwest from Cherokee to the even more tourist-traveled Gatlinburg and Pigeon Forge in Tennessee. The road winds steeply through dense forests packed with magnificent giant hardwoods, flowering poplar, dogwood, azalea, and rhododendron, and evergreen pines and firs at the highest elevations. Where the highway reaches the crest, a spur road runs parallel to the Appalachian Trail five miles west to 6,642-foot **Clingman's Dome,** the highest point in the park, where you can take a short but steep trail up to a lookout tower.

One of the most extensive natural areas—unlogged, old-growth forest, full of the park's oldest and tallest trees—lies at the very center of the park, off Newfound Gap Road on the north side of the crest. Starting at the popular Chimney Tops picnic area, the well-marked, three-quarter-mile **Cove Hardwood nature trail** winds through a sampling of the park's most stately maples and other broad-leafed trees—the ones responsible for the best of the fall colors.

Biologists estimate that some 500 native **black bears** live in the backcountry (and campgrounds!) of Great Smoky Mountains National Park.

The Appalachian Trail runs along the crest of the Great Smoky Mountains, crossing **Newfound Gap Road** at the center of the park. West of the park, the AT crosses another great road, US-129, whose winding route takes in more than 300 twisty corners in less than 12 miles. Dubbed the "Tail of the Dragon," this one of the country's great driving (and motorcycling) routes.

Along Little River Road, west of the Sugarlands Visitor Center off US-441 at the park's northern entrance, stands another group of ancient trees. Midway along, trails lead to two marvelous waterfalls, Laurel Falls

The many different **salamanders** native to the Great Smokies range from the tiny pygmy to the massive hellbender, which grows up to two feet long, head to tail. These crawling critters have earned the Great Smokies a reputation as the Salamander Capital of the World.

and Meigs Falls. Little River Road ends up at **Cades Cove,** where the preserved remnants of a mountain community that existed here from the early 1800s until the 1930s give a strong sense of Appalachian folk ways. A church and a number of mills still stand, and interpretive staff offer guided walks and other programs explaining the history and culture of these "hillbilly" people—some 6,000 of whom used to live within the park boundaries. **Bike rentals** are available at the Cades Cove campground, and you'll find plenty of opportunities for rides along the old country lanes.

Just over the mountains on the Tennessee side of the Great Smokies, Dolly Parton owns, runs, and stars at **Dollywood** (800/DOLLYWOOD), the country's biggest autobiographical theme park.

Another popular park destination is **Grotto Falls,** southeast of Gatlinburg via the Roaring Fork Road, where a short, flat trail to the tumbling cascade leads through lush hemlock forest—an ideal environment for mushrooms, and for the 27 different species of salamanders that slither around underfoot.

The only beds available in the park are at the historic **LeConte Lodge** (865/429-5704), built in the 1920s atop 6,593-foot Mt. LeConte, and located a six-mile hike from the nearest road. There are no phones, no TVs, little privacy, and no indoor plumbing, but the $115 and up nightly rates do come with "family-style" breakfast and dinner. Ten fairly basic **campgrounds** (no showers or hookups) operate in the park, with reservations taken only for the largest and most popular ones at Cades Cove, Elkmont, and Smokemount (800/365-2267). These three are accessible to RVs up to 35 feet long; for hikers, there are also bear-proofed backcountry shelters along the Appalachian Trail.

For more information, or to pick up the handy brochures ($0.35 each) describing the park's array of flora, fauna, trails, and other features, stop by either of the two main visitors centers. North of Cherokee at the south entrance, the **Oconaluftee Visitor Center** (828/497-1900) stands alongside a restored pioneer farmstead, where crafts demonstrations are given in summer. From the **Sugarlands Visitor Center** (865/436-1200), two miles south of Gatlinburg, Tennessee, you can take a short hike to Cataract Falls.

South to Georgia: Franklin

South from Cherokee and the Great Smoky Mountains, US-441 runs through the giant **Nantahala National Forest,** which stretches all the way to the Georgia border. It's a fast road, mostly divided, four-lane freeway, passing through a fairly developed corridor of towns and small cities.

The biggest town in this part of North Carolina, **Franklin** (pop. 3,490) was founded in the mid-1800s on a shallow ridge overlooking the Little Tennessee River. Along with lumber milling, Franklin's main industry has long been the mining of gemstones—garnets, rubies, and sapphires. Now a light industrial center, spread out around the intersection of US-441 and US-64, Franklin has a compact downtown area packed with gemstone and jewelry shops like **Ruby City,** 130 E. Main Street, which also has a small free museum. The **Franklin Motel** ($60; 828/524-4431 or 800/433-5507), at 17 W. Palmer Street, has clean, comfortable rooms and a swimming pool.

US-441 races south to Georgia from Franklin, while Hwy-28/US-64 heads southeast through the heart of **Transylvania County,** known as the "Land of Waterfalls" because of its many cascades. The biggest of these is 13 miles from Franklin and named, for some unknown reason, **Dry Falls.** From the

One of the few radio stations you can hear in mountainous western North Carolina, Franklin's **WPFJ 1480 AM** plays an entertaining combination of local news and contemporary Christian country music.

Between Franklin and Highlands, US-64 passes by several waterfalls and has been designated a Mountain Waters Scenic Byway.

Detour: Chattanooga

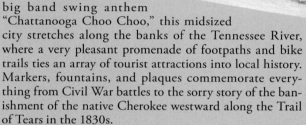

Mixing traditional southern hospitality with fascinating history, cultural vitality, and a stupendous natural setting, Chattanooga is an unexpected treat. Best known to older generations as the home base of Glenn Miller's 1940s big band swing anthem "Chattanooga Choo Choo," this midsized city stretches along the banks of the Tennessee River, where a very pleasant promenade of footpaths and bike trails ties an array of tourist attractions into local history. Markers, fountains, and plaques commemorate everything from Civil War battles to the sorry story of the banishment of the native Cherokee westward along the Trail of Tears in the 1830s.

The opening of the ever-expanding **Tennessee Aquarium** (daily; $22; 423/265-0698), one of the largest and most popular in the country, was key to Chattanooga's current renaissance. Along with an **IMAX theater,** the excellent **Hunter Art Museum,** and a minor league baseball stadium, the aquarium has energized a

well-signed parking area, follow a short trail that ends up underneath and behind the impressively raging torrent, a powerful white-noise generator you can hear long before you reach it. Another waterfall, known as **Bridal Veil Falls,** is a mile south from Dry Falls.

Two miles south from Bridal Veil Falls, US-64 enters the resort community of **Highlands** (pop. 900). Here Hwy-106 loops back to the southwest, giving grand panoramic views over the forested foothills before rejoining US-441 across the Georgia border in Dillard.

GEORGIA

If Georgia brings to mind endless, flat cotton or peanut plantations, you'll be pleasantly surprised by the mountainous wholesale reconstruction of the Chattanooga riverfront. On a nice summer's day, cross the river on the 110-year-old **Walnut Street Bridge,** gazing down at kayakers and rock climbers before hopping on the dollar-a-ride historic carousel in idyllic **Coolidge Park.**

While the aquarium and related attractions have given the city a new lease on life, one of the country's most enduring tourist attractions, **Rock City,** has been tempting travelers here for nearly a century. Standing six miles south of town atop 2,000-foot-tall **Lookout Mountain,** Rock City is one of the most hyped sights in the United States. From the 1930s through the 1960s, hundreds of rural barns from Michigan to Texas were painted with the words "See Rock City," "World's 8th Wonder," and "See 7 States." (The claim that one can see seven states from Rock City is disputed, but in order of distance they would be Georgia, Tennessee, Alabama, North Carolina, South Carolina, Kentucky, and Virginia.) **Rock City** (423/821-2544) itself is terrific, with paths winding through oddly shaped limestone canyons at the edge of heart-stopping cliffs. Even better are the other attractions atop Lookout Mountain, especially the beautiful limestone caves, the 150-foot-high underground **Ruby Falls,** and the historic **Incline Railroad.** Each attraction costs around $15, and all-inclusive tickets are available.

wilds of the state's northern tier. The great Appalachian ridge that runs along the East Coast has its southern foot here, high up in the forests of Rabun County, which packs natural wonders, outdoor adventures, and down-home Appalachian spirit into the state's small, isolated corner. Chattooga River white water—made famous by the movie *Deliverance,* and rated among the top 10 river runs in the United States—is the biggest draw, and sightseers can take in the spectacular waterfalls of Chattooga's Tallulah Gorge. Christmas-tree farms, dairies, and car graveyards dot the old-time mountain towns, but the ongoing "improvement" of US-441 into a four-lane freeway has resulted in a development boom of golf courses and mountain-view estates, increasing exponentially as the route approaches Atlanta's endless suburbs.

Dillard

Just south of the North Carolina border, the highway hamlet of **Dillard** (pop. 199) is a mini fiefdom of the Dillard family, whose name dates back to the 1700s in these parts. For generations, the Dillards have run a

local hospitality empire based around the sprawling set of bungalows, lodges, and dining rooms all going by the name **Dillard House** (706/746-5348), on a hill above US-441 at the south edge of town. Heading up the complex is the Dillard House restaurant, famous for its all-you-can-eat country cooking and its glass-walled patio, where diners can enjoy plates of classic country ham, fried chicken, pan-fried trout, vegetables, cornbread, and assorted relishes and desserts. The legendary institution may today impress you as more institution than legend—bus tours dominate the clientele—but you never leave hungry. Rooms ($80 and up) are around back in low-slung lodges scattered near a swimming pool, tennis courts, and a petting zoo.

In addition to the rambling inn, the family oligarchy operates a row of roadside businesses off US-441, selling collectible and keepsake souvenirs.

The hikers' Appalachian Trail crosses the Georgia/North Carolina border roughly 10 miles west of Dillard, then veers southeast, coming to a finale at the 3,782-foot summit of **Springer Mountain,** where a photogenic sign marks the end (or the beginning, since most of the 200 or so annual through-hikers travel south to north) of the 2,144-mile trail.

Black Rock Mountain State Park

At the wind-worn summit of 3,640-foot Black Rock Mountain, a flagstone terrace looks out over a grand Appalachian panorama: If there's no fog, you can see clear to the South Carolina Piedmont 80 miles away and as far as the Great Smokies to the north. The highest state park in Georgia, **Black Rock Mountain State Park** offers hiking trails and accommodations in addition to the splendid vistas. Set off in a ring at the top of the mountain, 10 spacious cot-

tages are removed from lowland civilization—no phones, no TVs, just fireplaces
and porch rockers. The cottages cost
around $125 a night, sleep up to 10 people,
and are available for rent year-round—a
nice snowy winter retreat. There's also a
pair of campgrounds. The park is three

> The rocky crest of Black
> Rock Mountain marks the
> eastern **Continental
> Divide**—from here waters
> part to follow a path to
> either the Atlantic Ocean
> or the Gulf of Mexico.

miles north of Clayton, well signed to the west of US-441. For information, or for reservations for the cabins or the campgrounds,
contact the **visitors center** (706/746-2141) near the summit.

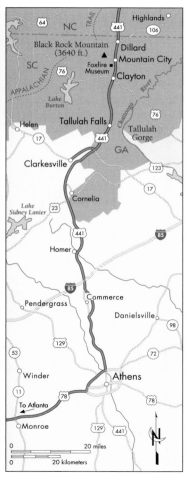

Mountain City: Foxfire Museum

The monolith of Black Rock
Mountain imposes an early
twilight on **Mountain City**
(pop. 784), the community
that stretches along US-441.
Tucked away on the west side
of US-441 just south of the
turnoff to Black Mountain
State Park, the modest
Foxfire Museum (Mon.–
Sat.; $6; 706/746-5828) is
part of a radical cultural and
educational movement that
began here in the mid-1960s
when local schoolteacher
Eliot Wigginton, frustrated
in attempts to motivate his
uninspired high-school students, assigned them the task
of interviewing their elders
about how things were in "the
old days." The students, inspired with the newly discov-
ered richness of their
Appalachian heritage, assembled the written interviews
into a magazine, which they
named *Foxfire* after a lumi-
nescent local fungus.

The magazine expanded

Atlanta

With a youthful and energetic metropolitan population rapidly approaching three million people, Atlanta has emerged as one of the most dynamic communities in the country. State capital of Georgia, and world headquarters of that flagship of American culture, Coca-Cola, Atlanta is the financial and cultural heart of the "New South," having recovered from its total destruction during the Civil War. Despite the sprawling scale of the place, in general people here are gracious and welcoming, so much so they could seem like walking parodies of Southern hospitality—if they weren't so darn sincere.

Atlanta began as a railroad junction (its original name was simply "Terminus"), and the early streetscape has been preserved and restored in **Underground Atlanta,** a warren of shop fronts underneath the center of the modern city. Abandoned in the 1920s, the buildings here were restored in the late 1980s to form a successful shopping and entertainment district. Numerous plaques and artworks commemorate the area's past, while two blocks to the east stands the gold-domed Georgia state capitol. On the northwest edge of downtown, building on the mixed success of the 1996 Olympics, Atlanta has developed Centennial Park as its new center, opening the $200 million **Georgia Aquarium** (daily; $30; 404/581-4000), the world's largest aquarium, alongside a showcase for the city's most successful product, **World of Coca Cola** (daily; $15; 800/676-

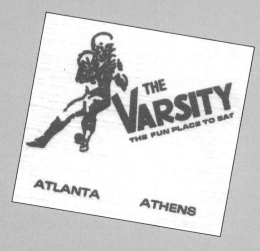

COKE). The surrounding area holds the world headquarters of another Atlanta product, CNN, along with the city's huge Georgia World Congress convention center, the Georgia Dome sports arena, and the campus of Georgia Tech university.

On the southwest side of downtown, near the I-20/I-85 junction, the powerhouse **Atlanta Braves** (800/326-4000) play at Turner Field, a.k.a. "The Ted."

Across the wide I-75 freeway, a half mile east of downtown, the **Martin Luther King Jr. National Historic Site** (daily; free; 404/331-5190), at 450 Auburn Avenue, sits at the heart of the predominantly black "Sweet Auburn" neighborhood. The four-block area holds many important landmarks in the life of Dr. King: his birthplace at 501 Auburn Avenue; the recently renovated Ebenezer Baptist Church, 407 Auburn Avenue, where he, his father, and his grandfather all served as pastor; and his tomb, emblazoned with the words "Free at Last, Free at Last," sitting on the grounds of the Center for Non-Violent Social Change, 449 Auburn Avenue.

Atlanta's main museum district is six miles north of downtown, in the upscale Buckhead neighborhood, where the **Atlanta History Center** (daily; $15; 404/814-4000), at 130 W. Paces Ferry Road, is a don't-miss introduction to the city, the state, and "The South" in general.

Practicalities

Atlanta's airport, Hartsfield International, one of the busiest in the country, is a dozen miles south of downtown Atlanta, at the junction of the I-85 and I-285 freeways. The usual rental cars, taxis and shuttle vans are supplemented by the extensive network of Metro Atlanta Rapid Transit Authority (MARTA) trains. The I-75 freeway cuts through the center of Atlanta, while the I-20 freeway skirts its southern edge. Sliced by freeways and spreading Los Angeles–like in a low-level ooze of mini malls, housing tracts, and traffic jams, Atlanta's outlying areas are impossible to make sense of, but the downtown area is compact and manageable. Note also that seemingly every

continued on next page

Atlanta (continued)

other thoroughfare includes the word "Peachtree" in its name, so check twice before getting completely lost.

Midtown Atlanta has a couple of nice places to stay, including the **Hotel Indigo** ($139 and up; 404/874-9200), at 683 Peachtree Street NE, a historic 1920s building upgraded into boutique status by the InterContinental chain, in a handy location across from the landmark Fox Theatre. The adjacent all-suite **Georgian Terrace** ($185 and up; 404/897-1991), at 659 Peachtree Street NE, is characterful and spacious.

East of the Midtown neighborhood, about two miles northeast of downtown, the lively Virginia-Highland district has Atlanta's best range of restaurants, cafés, and bars. There are also some older Atlanta landmarks, like **Mary Mac's Tea Room,** 224 Ponce de Leon Avenue (404/876-1800), serving traditional Southern food (fried chicken, peach cobbler, and sweet iced tea) since 1945. The same street also holds the **Majestic Diner,** 1031 Ponce de Leon Avenue (404/875-0276), a large, lively (and just a little bit seedy) 1940s-style café, open 24 hours for great waffles, burgers, and endless cups of java.

One more north-of-downtown Atlanta landmark deserves mention: **The Varsity** (404/881-1706), at 61 North Avenue near Georgia Tech alongside I-75, is the world's largest drive-in, serving up very good junk food: chili dogs, onion rings, and more Coca-Cola than anywhere else on this earth. Farther north, off I-85, carnivores and blues fans flock to **Fat Matt's Rib Shack** (404/607-1622) at 1811 Piedmont Avenue NE, while the **Colonnade,** 1879 Cheshire Bridge Road NE (404/874-5642), has been serving Southern food (baked ham, fried chicken, and more) since 1962.

After dark, enjoy an alfresco movie at the **Starlight Six** ($7, $1 for children under 10; 404/627-5786), four miles southeast of downtown at 2000 Moreland Avenue SE. Double features are shown every night, rain or shine, starting around 9 PM.

The usual barrage of tourist information can be had from the **Atlanta Convention and Visitors Bureau,** 233 Peachtree Street NE (800/ATLANTA).

to a series of *Foxfire* books, and more than eight million copies have been sold worldwide. The program's twofold success—educational innovation and folk-life preservation—further broadened as the then-emerging back-to-the-land movement seized upon these books as vital how-to manuals for subsistence farming and generally living off the grid. The Foxfire organization still runs classes and summer programs on a 110-acre campus in the hills above town.

Deliverance: Clayton

Slicing through the Appalachian wilderness along the Georgia–South Carolina border, the Chattooga River rates among the nation's top 10 white-water river adventures, attracting some 100,000 visitors a year for rafting, canoeing, kayaking, tubing, swimming, fishing, and riverside hiking. The Wild and Scenic–designated river was seen in the movie *Deliverance,* based on the book by Georgia poet and novelist James Dickey; ever since the movie was released, authorities have been pulling bodies out of the river—not toothless mountaineers but overconfident river-runners who underestimate the white water's power.

The largest town in the area, the down-home mountain community of **Clayton** (pop. 2,019) is a popular base for excursions into the wild forest and Chattooga River areas. US-441 has grown into an exurban morass of Wal-Mart sprawl, but Main Street, a three-block length of wooden storefronts on a sunny rise just west of US-411, still looks like you could hitch a horse at the curb without attracting much attention.

Tallulah Falls and Gorge

Balanced precariously over the precipitous gorge that once held the thundering cascades of the Tallulah River, tiny **Tallulah Falls** (pop. 147) has an illustrious history. As word of the natural wonder spread, crowds were drawn to the breathtaking sight, and by the turn of the century Tallulah Falls was a fashionable resort, with several elite hotels and boardinghouses catering to lowland sightseers. Fortunes changed when the falls were harnessed for hydroelectricity, but recent compromises have brought the falls back to occasional life. On

When you take in the sight of Tallulah Gorge, imagine walking a tightrope suspended 1,200 feet above the ground across its breadth. **"Professor Leon"** managed it (despite a stumble) in 1886, and in 1970, the flying **Karl Wallenda** replicated the feat, walking across on a wire suspended from the Tallulah Point Overlook, where postcards and photos document his effort.

weekends, usually in spring and fall, the waters are again released and can be admired from **Tallulah Gorge State Park** (706/754-7970), a very pleasant park with a local history museum, camping, showers, hiking trails, and a very cool suspension bridge over the river and gorge.

Stretching downstream along the six cascades of Tallulah Falls, the dramatic sheer walls of Tallulah Gorge have both haunted and attracted people for centuries. The wary Cherokee heeded legends that warriors who ventured in never returned, and many a curious settler had a waterfall or pool named in his honor—posthumously, after an untimely slip.

Tallulah Gorge is best seen via staircase-trails leading from the state park, or from the mile-long scenic route (old US-441), which loops off east of the modern highway. Drivers can pull over at numerous parking areas and take one of several rough trails along the gorge's rim, though the best views are from the historic **Tallulah Point Overlook** (daily 9 AM–6 PM; free), a privately owned concession stand midway along the loop.

Clarkesville

The charming little town of **Clarkesville** (pop. 1,248) retains a sophistication dating back to its founding over 150 years ago by lowland Carolina and coastal Georgian plantation families seeking refuge from the oppressive summer heat. Best known as the home of the renowned country resort Glen-Ella Springs Inn, Clarkesville sits at the lower slope of a river valley that stretches northwest to the faux-Bavarian town of Helen and is surrounded by countryside perfect for a leisurely drive or bike tour past an old mill here, a covered bridge there, and old-time country stores in wooden cabins.

In the mountains northwest of Clarkesville, 15 miles along Hwy-17 and Hwy-75, the tiny town of **Helen** (pop. 355) turned itself into a tourist draw in 1969 by remodeling all the buildings in mock-Bavarian decor and repaving the streets in cobblestones.

Clarkesville tucks urbane delights into its rustic country setting, with over 40 buildings, most of them former summer homes, listed on the National Register of Historic Places. Downtown, three blocks of wooden storefronts, centering on a shaded plaza where numerous festivals take place, hold cafés and crafts shops.

Hundred-year-old **Glen-Ella Springs Inn** ($125 and up; 706/754-7295), eight miles north of Clarkesville on Bear Gap Road off US-441, is northern Georgia's premier country inn. Set on 17 lush acres, the historic two-story lodge holds 16 guest rooms, each of which opens to a porch with rocking chairs.

Athens

If you've got the time and inclination, one of Georgia's most enjoyable destinations is just a slight veer to the east off our route: Athens, the coolest college town in the South. Famed for its lively music scene, which gave the world the alternative-rock bands B-52s and R.E.M., Athens is the home of the University of Georgia, whose

Cornelia, the southernmost Appalachian town, is known for its **Giant Apple Monument** on Hwy-23 downtown, and if you're here in fall you can sample them fresh from the tree.

Greek Revival campus sits at the center of town, bordered on the north by a half dozen blocks of cafés, bars, and book and record stores. Besides the dozens of super-sized Bulldogs (the UGA mascot) around town, Athens also holds a classic Road Trip destination: **"The Tree That Owns Itself,"** a second-generation mighty oak tree standing on a small circle of land at the corner of Finley and Dearing Streets west of campus, whose legal autonomy earned it a place in *Ripley's Believe or Not!*.

The main music venue is the **40 Watt Club** (706/549-7871), at 285 W. Washington Street, where R.E.M. played their second gig. Good, cheap food is available on the east side of town at **Weaver D's Soul Food BBQ** (706/353-7797), at 1016 E. Broad Street, whose enigmatic slogan "Automatic for the People" was enshrined as an R.E.M. album title. R.E.M.'s Michael Stipe owns gourmet vegetarian restaurant **The Grit** (706/543-6592) at 199 Prince Avenue. The best restaurant in Athens, and one of the top ten in the USA according to *Food & Wine Magazine,* is the **Five & Ten** (706/546-7300), at 1653 S. Lumpkin Street, off Milledge Street southwest of downtown. The Five & Ten is open for dinner nightly and Sunday brunch, serving a range of Southern favorites enlivened by inventive, international touches. (Fried catfish and grits with lemon and arugula, anyone?)

On to Atlanta: Stone Mountain

From the foothills of northern Georgia, it's only an hour by freeway southwest to Atlanta, the cultural and commercial center of the New South, and a fascinating (and fun) place to explore. Unfortunately, Atlanta is surrounded by miles and miles of mega-freeway sub-prime-mortgage sprawl, so you'll have to endure some of the country's craziest driving to get there.

From Athens, Hwy-316 merges into I-85 for the quickest route there, but for a more interesting route follow old US-78 southeast, approaching Atlanta by way of **Stone Mountain,** 16 miles east of downtown. A Confederate Mt. Rushmore and historic KKK rallying point, Stone Mountain (daily; $10 per car; 770/498-5690 or 800/401-2407) consists of the 20-times-larger-than-life figures of Robert E. Lee, "Stonewall" Jackson, and Jefferson Davis carved into an 800-foot-high hump of granite. A 45-minute patriotic laser-and-fireworks extravaganza is shown nightly in summer (May–late August). At the base of Stone Mountain are 3,200 acres of the tackier tourist traps going (riverboat cruises, a scenic railroad, a reconstructed antebellum plantation, a cable car Skylift to the summit, and a treetop "Sky Hike" rope course and rock-climbing complex—all of which charge separate fees of around $9 each, or $26 for an unlimited day pass. Also here are restaurants and hotels, plus and Atlanta's best campground.

Index

Photo and Illustration Credits

Road Trip USA and the Avalon Travel logo are the property of Avalon Travel, a member of the Perseus Books Group. All other photos, marks and logos depicted are the property of the original owners. All rights reserved.

All vintage postcards, photographs and maps in this book from the private collection of Jamie Jensen, unless otherwise credited.

Photos © Jamie Jensen: pages 27, 29, 30, 33, 34

United States Quarter-Dollar Coin Images
State quarter-dollar coin images from the United States Mint. Used with permission.

United States Postage Stamps
All postage stamps © United States Postal Service. All rights reserved. Used with permission. Written authorization from the Postal Service is required to use, reproduce, post, transmit, distribute, or publicly display these images.

Pages 7, 24, 37, 48, 52, 57, 73, 75, 77, 92, 107 Greetings from America Series Stamp Designs © 2002 United States Postal Service; page 17 Robert Frost © United States Postal Service

Additional Credits:
Page 9 © David Brownell/NHOTTD; 18 © Priscilla Carton/Clark's Trading Post; 45 printed by permission of the Norman Rockwell Family Agency, © 1960 the Norman Rockwell Family Entities; 326 © Ben Thompson; 61 photo supplied by, and reproduced with the permission of, Binney & Smith, maker of Crayola products.; 62, 86 (Prints and Photographs Division cph cph 3a55007); 63 © National Archives; 78 © Julian Smith; 91 courtesy of The Library of Congress; 92 © Mayberry Motor Inn; 104 courtesy of Dollywood; 106 courtesy of Steve Freer, Tennessee Valley Railroad Museum; 111 © Major League Baseball Association, courtesy of the Atlanta Braves

Cover Images:
Cover postcards from the private collections of Domini Dragoone, Jamie Jensen, and Kevin Roe. For original publisher information, see *Road Trip USA,* 5th edition (Avalon Travel, 2009).

Ready to hit the open road?

Visit **roadtripusa.com** for trip ideas, maps, road trip routes, a Driver's Almanac of monthly trip suggestions, and more.

Web-exclusive features include Jamie Jensen's Road Tripper blog and free downloadable podcasts.

roadtripusa.com—the online source for road trippers!

www.moon.com

DESTINATIONS | ACTIVITIES | BLOGS | MAPS | BOOKS

MOON.COM is ready to help plan your next trip! Filled with fresh trip ideas and strategies, author interviews, informative travel blogs, a detailed map library, and descriptions of all the Moon guidebooks, Moon.com is all you need to get out and explore the world—or even places in your own backyard. While at Moon.com, sign up for our monthly e-newsletter for updates on new releases, travel tips, and expert advice from our on-the-go Moon authors. As always, when you travel with Moon, expect an experience that is uncommon and truly unique.

MOON IS ON FACEBOOK—BECOME A FAN!
JOIN THE MOON PHOTO GROUP ON FLICKR

ROAD TRIP USA
Appalachian Trail
1st Edition

Jamie Jensen

Avalon Travel
a member of the Perseus Books Group
1700 Fourth Street
Berkeley, CA 94710, USA
www.avalontravelbooks.com

Printing History
1st edition — April 2010
5 4 3 2 1

Printed in the United States by RR Donnelley

ISBN: 978-1-59880-579-6
ISSN: 2152-3711

Editors: Kevin McLain, Elizabeth Hollis Hansen
Copy Editor: Valerie Sellers Blanton
Graphics Coordinator: Jane Musser
Production Coordinator: Darren Alessi
Map Editor: Mike Morgenfeld
Cartographers: Mike Morgenfeld, Kat Bennett
Proofreaders: Kia E. Wang, Nikki Iokimedes
Indexer: Judy Hunt